Juvenile Justice and Schools

Juvenile Justice and Schools

POLICING, PROCESSING, AND PROGRAMMING

First Edition

Written and edited by Doshie Piper, J. Renee Trombley,
Katalin Parti, Georgen Guerrero, O. Oko Elechi

cognella®
SAN DIEGO

Bassim Hamadeh, CEO and Publisher
John Remington, Executive Editor
Gem Rabanera, Senior Project Editor
Christian Berk, Production Editor
Emely Villavicencio, Senior Graphic Designer
Trey Soto, Licensing Coordinator
Natalie Piccotti, Director of Marketing
Kassie Graves, Vice President of Editorial
Jamie Giganti, Director of Academic Publishing

3970 Sorrento Valley Blvd., Ste. 500, San Diego, CA 92121

Contents

ACTIVE LEARNING

Throughout the text, when you see this Active Learning icon:

an interactive activity is available to complement your reading.

Your instructor may have customized the selection of activities available for your unique course. Please check with your professor to verify whether your class will access this content through the Cognella Active Learning portal (http://active.cognella.com) or through your home learning management system.

Acknowledgments

WE WOULD LIKE to thank our families and close friends who endured us through the creation of this text. Your sacrifices are not unnoticed.

We would also like to thank Dr. Elizabeth K. Englander for her feedback as a peer reviewer. Your content suggestions were greatly appreciated.

Cognella gratefully acknowledges the contributions of the following reviewers:

Nabil Ouassini, PhD
Assistant Professor
Prairie View A&M College of Juvenile Justice and Psychology

Elizabeth Englander, PhD
Executive Director
Massachusetts Aggression Reduction Center (MARC)
Bridgewater State University

Introduction

THE AUDIENCE FOR Juvenile Justice in Schools: Policing, Processing, and Programming is students enrolled in undergraduate programs in criminal justice, criminology, or juvenile justice. Teacher education programs can also use this text as an induction component for graduates during their first three years of teaching, which address three main areas: induction support, professional development, and professional networking. This book could be used as a part of any degree program to assist in professional development in the areas of juvenile justice in schools and classroom behavior management. This text can be used in both criminal justice and education to unpack this relationship between school and justice-involved youth.

The purpose of this text is to explore the intersection of juvenile justice and schools. This text explains the complex relationship between schools and the juvenile justice system. The data on low school performance and delinquency, truancy and juvenile court processing, and the school-to-prison pipeline are explored in depth and specifically in connection with juvenile court involvement. This book outlines the educational system involvement in the initiation and thus processing of the justice system involved youth and should teach undergraduate students about this interaction. It should also empower future juvenile practitioners, teachers, and administrators to implement and use available resources other than police or justice systems involvement in response to behavioral concerns.

The book is organized in chapters. Each chapter covers an overview of the topic and shows how that topic intersects with school systems and juvenile justice systems. Some chapters have images and figures that provide visual imagery to the topic. Other chapters have Quick Response (QR) codes that direct readers to specific sources or articles on the subject matter discussed. All in all, it is our hope that the readers of this text will feel engaged with the research on juveniles in the educational context in various ways.

CHAPTER ONE

Juveniles and Schools

HISTORICAL AND CONTEMPORARY PERSPECTIVES

Doshie Piper, J. Renee Trombley, and Danielle J. Alsandor

READING OBJECTIVES

- Understand the social construction of age in the educational setting.
- Identify the juvenile court's authority in the educational setting.
- Identify the significance of historical case law precedent in educational settings.
- Define and explain the legal rights of juveniles over time.

OVERVIEW

The primary role of schools is to educate students; however, they are also responsible for student discipline, operational policies and procedures, and law compliance. Schools are governed by policies and procedures. Usually, a governmental agency operated by the state oversees educational compliance. These institutions are responsible for ensuring schools' policies and procedures adhere to the legal code. They are responsible for maintaining their students' individual and educational rights. This can be a difficult task when considering the purpose, function, and operation of schools.

The many responsibilities schools have to fulfill place them in a difficult position when interacting with delinquent students. Schools have to comply with policies and procedures, and school officials have to administer discipline for policy violations that do not undermine students' rights. This is especially important when responding to student behavioral concerns that may be delinquent—that is, behavior that is prohibited because of age, such as not attending school, or behavior that violates a criminal code, such as theft. Schools must consider the constitutional rights of their students when responding. In addition, there is a need to consider the long-term impact and implications of the educational interaction on students' futures. Despite students' delinquent status, juveniles have some fundamental rights in public schools. Likewise, schools have a fundamental right the keep everyone safe and promote a learning environment. Some schools have adopted rigid and intrusive security measures that diminish the rights of students (Beger, 2002). Instead of protecting schoolchildren from arbitrary police intrusion, courts have given law enforcement officers the widest latitude with students (Beger, 2002).

CONCEPTUALIZING AGE IN EDUCATION

Age serves many purposes. It determines when individuals start school, vote, and consume tobacco and alcohol. Chronological age marks developmental time as a simple index of the stage in the process of growing older. Chronological age is a determining factor for school readiness, and this has presented some challenges to the educational system because of the fluidity of age or stratification of age. Age stratification is socially recognized divisions within society that identify appropriate behaviors by grouping. Norms, expectations, privileges, and constraints express societal distinctions regarding age—for example, the appropriate time to begin school is during childhood. It would be inappropriate for an infant or toddler to attend primary school. Developmental age also plays a role in determining the appropriate time to begin school—the time at which learning and cognition begin. This may present a layer of complexity to schools when faced with exercising criminal law and procedure in the school context and the social construction of age.

Psychological age is how old someone feels, acts, and behaves, and it does not necessarily equal chronological age, which is the age since birth (Kolodinsky, Cranwell, & Rowe, 2002). An individual can therefore have a psychological age that exceeds their chronological age if they are mature, or at least feel older than they really are. For example, this may be common in adolescence when young teens that feel older than they really are engage in behaviors typical of late teens and early adults. There is some indication that social maturity and achievement motivation in teens could be associated with an advanced psychological age which is said to be associated with a parenting environment that is authoritative, emotionally warm, democratic, and firm. The same is true for the inverse, when someone is psychologically or developmental immature. There are salient features of adolescent development that contribute to the conceptualization of psychological age. These are normative developmental changes that occur over time during a youth's adolescent years and distinguish adolescents from children or from adults (Grisso & Schwartz, 2000). These changes are most relevant to the treatment of young people within the juvenile justice system. These changes occur across four distinct but interrelated domains: physical, intellectual, emotional, and social.

- Physical Development—Physical changes of adolescence that take place during puberty transform the adolescent's appearance in dramatic ways. The most important changes include the appearance of secondary sex characteristics, increases in muscle mass, and changes in the shape and characteristics of the face. Factors include puberty hormones (an increase in the secretion of growth hormones), sexual development, and greater impulsiveness.
- Intellectual Development—A second salient aspect of adolescent development concerns the growth of intellectual abilities. Adolescents have less future orientation. They have less ability to conceive the future and less anticipation of consequences. When compared to children, adolescents tend to think in ways that are more advanced, abstract, efficient, and effective. Although the raw intellectual abilities of older adolescents are comparable to adults, young people may have less experience to draw on than adults. They are more risk averse. They seek instant gratification. They are less risk averse and inexperienced compared to adults.
- Emotional Development—Adolescents experience a time of emotional development. This is a time of change in the way individuals view themselves in their capacity to function independently. Factors include more emotional behavior, aggressiveness (boys), less self-esteem, self-criticism, self-control, and greater insecurity and self-discovery compared to adults. It has been shown that their self-esteem becomes stable from around age 13 onwards.
- Social Development—Social development during adolescence is marked by an increase in the importance of peers, the emergence of interest in romantic relationships, and the onset of sexual activity. Factors include more susceptibility to peer pressure, being less amenable to social control, and sexual development/boundaries (Grisso & Schwartz, 2000). Age in the legal context is the primary determinant of juvenile court jurisdiction, and this varies across states. Chronological age marks developmental time as a simple index of a stage in the process of growing older. The concept of old has changed over time; the life span of an adult male in 1500–1600 was around 30 years, now it is about 75–76 years (Elder, 1985). Social age focuses on the social meaning of age (Elder, 1985). Norms, expectations, privileges, and constraints express societal distinctions regarding age; for example, legal drinking age in the United States as opposed to Europe (Elder & Rockwell, 2010). Age strata are socially recognized divisions within society that identify appropriate behaviors. The state legislature determines who's a juvenile. It sets the upper and lower age limits. These are primarily between 7 and 17 years old (Elrod & Ryder, 2011). As a result, primary educational institutions have a responsibility to understand the various legal constructs of age and must ensure that when implementing disciplinary procedures, they comply with these legal constructs.

FOUNDATIONS OF JUVENILE JUSTICE INTERVENTION IN EDUCATION

The development of a separate processing system for juveniles was imperative. A separation in systems was important primarily to child advocates; however, others became concerned about juvenile treatment in the legal system. The adult system is focused on punishment, which calls for a separation of juvenile offenders based on this premise. Juvenile offenders are solely accountable and legally responsible for their actions, not how their actions affect others. Child advocates emphasize if youth are well-adjusted and if courts focus on care, treatment, and rehabilitation, they are working in the best interest of the child. Focusing on the best interest of the child is important for the majority of juvenile offenders (Lawrence & Hemmens et al., 2013). After numerous developments and 100 years in operation, the juvenile court system is still facing many obstacles.

Before the establishment of juvenile court, houses of refuge were used to respond to wayward youth. Youth who were out of school and street dependent were considered wayward. The most prominent care facilities developed by the Child Savers were the houses of refuge; the first was opened in New York in 1825. This institution was publicly supported by the state. It was also the first time an institution separated children from adults. Its concept of protecting potential delinquent youths was to take children off the streets and reform them in a family-like environment. Boston followed a year later and then Philadelphia in 1829. These houses of refuge were designed to maintain class status and prevent unrest.

The Quakers believed poverty eventually led to crime; impoverished children needed to be separated from their poor parents (or they would end up the same way); education along the lines of moral, vocational, and traditional instruction (i.e., reading, mathematics, and arithmetic) needed to be forced upon these children in order to break the cycle of poverty; and the state (as represented by the Quakers) was obliged to undertake these tasks (Sanborn & Salerno, 2005). The Quakers designed Houses of Refuge to operationalize these beliefs; they opened first in New York (1825), Boston (1826), and Philadelphia (1828) before expanding to the Midwest. Three categories of youths were subject to being incarcerated in the House of Refuge: (1) youths who were convicted of minor crimes in criminal court, (2) those found guilty of begging and conducting minor noncriminal disturbances, and (3) those who were sent there by their parents. The latter group represented an expansion of state's parens patriae power.

The Crouse case (named after the last name of the child) upheld the operation of the 19th-century reform schools as an effort led by the Quakers who had been upset with the incarceration of youth in penitentiaries with the hope that the right environment could actually help youth live meaningful lives. *Ex parte Crouse* (1839) allowed houses of refuge to intervene in the lives of youth. This case was known as the

Pennsylvania juvenile justice case in 1839 that took away the due process proceedings of the Bill of Rights from juveniles. It was the case of juvenile Mary Ann Crouse. Her mother gave the Philadelphia House of Refuge jurisdiction of Crouse. However, once Crouse's father learned she was living in the Philadelphia House of Refuge, he filed a *habeas corpus* against the Philadelphia House of Refuge to release his daughter to him. Yet, the court refused to release her based on the parens patriae. Ex parte Crouse set the precedent for parens patriae as it allowed the state to confine youth.

Parens patriae is the legal doctrine that allows the courts and the county to become the parent of the state or state as parents. This doctrine also allows the state to intervene and act in the best interest of the child whenever it deems necessary. This means that the parents' "legal rights over their children cease to exist by court order" (Curtis, 1976). Arguably, this interpretation of parens patriae would not have been possible if the Crouse decision had not already taken parens patriae a far distance from its source. In turn, this application of parens patriae would not likely have been possible unless the Crouse court had accepted the Quakers' vision of both the state as the ultimate parent for the purpose of state intervention. *Crouse* became the foundation for incarceration of youth in houses of refuge sent there by their parents. This critical case would not have the same success for the second category of youth sent to houses of refuge (those guilty of begging and minor noncriminal disturbances), as shown in the ruling of *People v. Turner* (1870).

In *People v. Turner* (1870), a boy named Daniel Turner was considered a "misfortunate," or someone who was in danger of becoming a delinquent because his family was poor and unable to care for him. He was remanded to the Chicago House of Refuge for vagrancy, not a delinquent act. His father filed a writ of habeas corpus, and the court ruled the state has no power to imprison a child, who has committed no crime, on the mere allegation that he is "destitute of proper parental care, and is growing up in mendicancy, ignorance, idleness, and vice" (*People ex rel. O'Connell v. Turner*, 1870). His parents won the case, and it was decided that the state should only intervene in troubled families given extreme circumstances. However, the verdict was largely ignored by the courts. Youths continued to be sent to Houses of Refuge for being guilty of begging and minor noncriminal disturbances.

However, the *Crouse* case became the foundation of the new juvenile court through *Commonwealth v. Fisher* (1905). In this case, Frank Fischer, a 14-year-old male was indicated for larceny and committed to the House of Refuge until his 21st birthday. His father objected at his placement and filed suit which argued his son's seven-year sentence was harsher than it would have been if he were sentenced in criminal court. The father lost his appeal and the Pennsylvania Supreme Court ruling was upheld. This, in turn, became the foundation for all other appellate courts in the country as they were asked if the juvenile courts in their states could operate without giving youths charged with crimes due process rights (Sanborn & Salerno, 2005). As juvenile courts spread throughout the United States, juveniles challenged the lack of constitutional rights. Virtually every state court decided that the state may intervene in families when the parents are unable to prevent their children from engaging in crime citing parens patriae and *Commonwealth v. Fisher* (Sanborn & Salerno, 2005). Furthermore, it ruled that due process protections were not necessary when the states were acting under parens patriae. This doctrine was the major construct for creating juvenile courts. This case never rose to the level of the U.S. Supreme Court; yet, it is precedent. The reasoning has prevailed throughout centuries. This case established the following:

1. *Parens patriae* and *in loco parentis* apply to all juvenile cases, and the state has the legal right to replace the biological parents and cut off all parental legal rights to their children.
2. Juvenile civil proceedings are not criminal proceedings and do not provide juveniles with the constitutional due process rights that adults possess.
3. Juvenile secure institutions are not prisons; instead, they are to be considered schools whose purpose is to reform wayward and troubled juveniles.

The term *in loco parentis*, Latin for "in the place of a parent" or "instead of a parent," refers to the legal responsibility of a person or organization to take on some of the functions and responsibilities of a parent. Originally derived from English common law, it is applied in two separate areas of the law. First, it allows institutions such as colleges and schools to act in the best interests of students as they see fit, although not allowing what would be considered violations of the students' civil liberties.

Second, this doctrine can allow a non-biological parent to be given the legal rights and responsibilities of a biological parent if they have held themselves out as the parent. The *in loco parentis* doctrine is distinct from the doctrine of *parens patriae*, the psychological parent doctrine, and adoption. In the United States, the parental liberty doctrine imposes constraints on the operation of the in loco parentis doctrine. Both of these legal premises gave way to the establishment of the juvenile court.

The Juvenile Court Act of 1899 authorized the first juvenile court established in Chicago. This legislation provided power over youth 16 years old or younger who engaged in delinquency and were dependent or neglected (Waegel, 1989). This new court was required to be overseen by a special judge; hearings were held in a separate courtroom and the records for juvenile court cases kept separate (Empey, Stafford, & Hay, 1982). Judge Julian Mack was the presiding judge. This court marked the formal beginning of a separate juvenile justice system, which was a new method to adjudicate or deal with juvenile offenders. The philosophy of the court was to rehabilitate juvenile offenders based on the medical model. By 1903, St. Louis, Missouri, established its juvenile court as depicted in Figure 1.1, where a small boy who was habitually truant was going before the juvenile court. Within 10 years, 10 other states

FIGURE 1.1 Juvenile Court. Small boy who was habitually truant. A street boy. Thursday, May 5, 1910. Location: St. Louis, Missouri

had established a juvenile court that closely followed the model developed in Chicago (Krisberg & Austin, 1993).

Juvenile court cases were closed and were not always held in courtrooms. As a matter of fact, it was preferred that juvenile hearings be held in offices instead of traditional courtrooms. These closed hearings were only open to individuals participating in the case: judges, parents, children, and probation officers. The juvenile court was procedurally informal and intended to serve the best interest of the children, so record keeping was not necessary. If records were kept, they were sealed and kept private. Guilt or innocence was not sought as the necessary outcome in juvenile court procedures because of the informal nature of court. *In re Winship* (see more in Chapter 7) was the case that stressed the rehabilitative nature of the juvenile court. The juvenile justice system was fundamentally designed to rehabilitate juveniles who were brought to its attention. An important component of any rehabilitative effort is the assessment provided to the court by the juvenile probation officer. The information attained by the probation officer in these interviews is very useful to the court as it attempts to individualize a disposition that will rehabilitate a juvenile who has come to its attention. Therefore, the due process protections that exist in the adult system do not apply to the juvenile court procedure. Judges exercised wide discretion intervening in youth lives over the actions they took. These discretionary actions ranged from stern warnings to placement in an institution (Bartollas & Miller, 2010).

EDUCATIONAL CONTEXT

Anyone paying attention to what is happening today in our schools could be quick to point out the landscape looks a lot different than it did just a few decades ago. Everything from classroom curriculum to cafeteria options has seen dramatic changes, and issues of student discipline to present concerns with school security are shaping the nation's children and their K-12 experiences. The practices of the educational system and the experiences of students in our schools will both affect the juvenile justice system, and, in turn, the juvenile justice system will affect the lives of students who become involved in the system through their experiences with institutions of education.

Understanding the development of public education can be beneficial, especially when we consider the fact that while many people believe strongly in the morality of offering public education, some scholars have argued that its development was not necessarily a purely altruistic movement. Platt (1977) and others have argued while advocating for the right to education for all, many of the projects related to juveniles were based on issues of control and dominance over lower class youth and their experiences and expectations. A capitalist country called for workers who were educated enough to serve as profitable employees in the working class. The policies and practices within public education have exemplified this fact over the last few decades.

Attending school in the United States during the K-12 years is not considered a luxury; in fact, it is mandatory, and this has a huge effect on the lives of our children and their families. According to the National Center for Education Statistics (NCES, n.d.), all 50 states and the District of Columbia each have some form of legislation that mandates school attendance guidelines for children. This legislation covers children ranging from the ages of 5 to 19 years old. Half of all states have compulsory attendance laws for children starting at 6 years of age and older, and the majority of the other states are nearly equally divided by attendance requirements starting at age 5 or 7 years, with only two states delaying this requirement for children until they reach age 8—that being the states of Pennsylvania and Washington (NCES, n.d.).

In addition, this report also notes that half of these states require compulsory education up until the age of 18, while 25 states set the upper age limit at 16 or 17 years old. Only one state, Texas, provides requirements for compulsory school attendance until a juvenile has reached the age of 19 (NCES, n.d.). Compulsory attendance laws are just one way that children and their families can end up dealing with police and the juvenile court system, but we will discuss this issue in more detail later.

According to NCES (n.d.), there were expectations for over 50 million students to be entering K-12 public schools in the fall semester of 2017. This represents a slight growth from the previous year and does not include another 5.2 million students who are expected to enroll in private schools. In addition, there are an estimated 20.4 million students expected to start college in 2017 (NCES, n.d.). Although most teachers are notoriously underpaid, and many public schools are typically underfunded, it is still easy to see that education is big business.

In 2011, the U.S. Census Bureau reported 77 million students in the United States, ages 3 years and older. According to their report, they estimate Americans spent close to $10 billion on back-to-school shopping, including clothing, accessories, and books. This does not even include the amount of money spent each year on technology as students go back to school. Items ranging from home computers, laptops, and notebooks, as well as new phones, expensive calculators, and specific computer software for use in education, also represent huge expenditures for families with students in the home.

When examining governmental spending on education, it is noted that on average, $10,499 was spent on each student in the United States. Utah is noted as spending the least amount of money on educating their children at only $6,356 allotted per student, and New York was named as spending the most, averaging $18,126 spent annually per student in that state (U.S. Census Bureau, 2019). Overall, total public school expenditures have reached more than $600 billion annually (Digest of Educational Statistics, 2012).

With education being such an important aspect of everyday life for our students, we must question the experiences of students across class, race, and gender lines. When we do, we find some of the same discriminatory practices within the justice system, and the results of these policies and practices have led to disproportionate characteristics and outcomes within the institution of education here in America.

According to the census, there were a projected 3.2 million students graduating with their high school diplomas in the 2011–2012 school year (U.S. Census Bureau, 2019). Yet, according to the NCES (n.d), although gaps have been decreasing over the years, percentages of students graduating by race are still not equally proportionate. In fact, there are continuing disparities. For instance, while the highest adjusted cohort graduation rate (ACGR) was reported in 2015–2016 at 84%, meaning that four out of every five students enrolled in ninth grade are completing their high school diplomas within 4 years, these rates varied considerably by race (NCES, n.d).

According to NCES (n.d.) Asian/Pacific Islanders had the highest completion rate at 91%, white youth were next at 88%, the Hispanic completion rate was listed at 79%, while black youth had an ACGR rate of 76%, and American Indians/Alaska Natives representing the group with the lowest completion rate of 72%. These statistics show disparities in educational attainment by race and lead us to broader questions regarding the experience of students in our school system. Specifically, the examination of additional statistics and disproportionality can help us successfully interpret what we see within our educational institutions.

We know a strong relationship exists between education, juvenile delinquency, and incarceration. In fact, education is known to have a huge effect on individual trajectories during the life course. Levels of education are known to affect quality of life variables, including those related to family and social life experiences, potential job opportunities, and associated income earnings over the lifetime, as well as all sorts of correlational risks, including those stemming from physical and mental health issues to those associated with arrests and incarceration.

SOCIAL CONTEXT OF SCHOOLS AND DELINQUENCY

Clearly, schools have a profound impact on youth lives. Students spend more awake hours in school than at home. This is in part because schools teach youths skills that are needed for participation in social and economic life. Less frequently discussed by educational institutions is the fact that schools serve other less obvious societal functions, including providing care while parents work; delaying entrance into the workforce; encouraging the development of social competencies; and building or maintaining established social roles (Weisner & Collins, 1984). Thus, the schooling process has a significant impact on the development of children both academically and societally. This suggests that schooling is an important factor in determining one's economic and social status.

However, many students do not experience success in school as noted above. School failure is directly tied to delinquency. Studies have shown that poor school performance, truancy, and leaving school at a young age are connected to juvenile delinquency (Bachman, Green, & Wirtanen, 1971; Elliott, 1978; Elliott & Voss, 1974; Farrington, 1986). In other words, students who fail in school are at the risk of delinquency. The factors related to school failure are lack of commitment to school, lack of attachment in school, and student alienation. For example, when a student comes to reject academic achievement and prosocial behavior as a legitimate goal, feelings of isolation begin to set in, and a student's perception that he or she is not receiving the necessary emotional support from caring adults (parents, teachers, and school administrators) plays a role in the onset of delinquent or aggressive behaviors (Gottfredson, 1997). School failure and delinquency are also related to social class.

There is an entire chapter on poverty and education achievement. Many lower socioeconomic status (SES) youths may lack the prerequisite skills for academic success (Elrod & Ryder, 2011). According to Buckingham, Wheldall, and Beaman-Wheldall (2013), youth from low-SES families are less likely to have experiences that encourage the development of fundamental skills of reading attainment, such as phonetic awareness, word recognition, and speech ability. Likewise, children's initial reading competency is correlated with the home literacy environment, number of books owned, and parent distress (Aikens & Barbarin, 2008). However, households at or below the federal poverty level have less access to learning materials and experiences, including books, computers, educational toys, skill-building lessons, or tutors to create a positive home learning environment (Bradley, Corwyn, McAdoo, & García Coll, 2001). Poverty in turn is a strong contributor to formation of delinquent subcultures, due to the rejection of mainstream educational attainment.

Albert Cohen (1955) proposed the subcultural theory which suggests delinquency is a consequence of young people coming together into the so-called subcultures where deviant values dominate. Subcultural theory became the dominant theory in the '50s and '60s. Cohen (1955) shows in subculture theory how boys from the lower socioeconomic class always strive to adapt to higher social strata but are confronted with goals they cannot achieve due to their socioeconomic background or rigid social structures. Cohen (1955) then compares these boys with middle-class boys. The low-SES boys must acknowledge their low status, poor prestige, and minimum chances of success in business and society. The resulting problems of self-respect ultimately lead to the merging of several such boys into alternative subgroups, which are defined by their separation from the middle class. Thus, leading youth to nonacademic or vocational tracks that they are still likely to experience the consequences of their school failure in.

Students that experience school failure are more likely to drop out and experience delinquency, which has negative consequences. Some of these negative consequences are diminished job prospects and difficulty meeting income needs; psychological and social consequences; personal dissatisfaction and regret; lower occupational aspirations; and lower educational aspirations for their children (Elrod & Ryder, 2011). School dropouts tend to be from low-SES groups, members of minority groups, from homes with fewer study aids, from single-parent homes or from homes with less parental supervision, more likely to get poor grades and low scores on achievement tests, less likely to be involved in extracurricular activities, and more likely to have discipline problems (Elrod & Ryder, 2011). The research on dropping out of school and delinquency has produced mixed results. Some research indicates delinquent behavior decreases after youths drop out. Other research studies indicate that youths' criminal activities increase after dropping out. Despite the ongoing debate of the relationship between dropping out and delinquency, the focus should be on school policies that reduce dropout rate by improving the ability to meet the needs of all students (Elrod & Ryder, 2011).

This text discusses the following points:

- Explores the intersection of juvenile justice and schools, as many youth enter the system from school referrals.
- Presents the data on low school performance and delinquency, truancy and juvenile court processing, and the school-to-prison pipeline.

- Explains the complex relationship between schools and the juvenile justice system. Youth are referred to juvenile courts for truancy, substance use, and other criminal offenses in schools.
- Outlines the educational system's involvement in the initiation and thus processing of youth in the justice system.
- Highlights both the criminal justice and education systems' methods of labeling and processing youth as delinquents.
- Explores how schools rely heavily on police and school resource officers.
- Presents proactive responses to school discipline, violence, and misbehavior through the five most popular school violence programs containing an anti-bullying component running in the United States today: the Olweus Bullying Prevention Program, Positive Action, Second Step, Steps to Respect, and KiVa. The description of the major content elements and the evaluation of the programs are to be included in a critical approach: what works and what is to be further developed in these programs to create a more secure and peaceful learning school environment. It sets up a standard for evaluation criteria as far as anti-bullying evaluative assessment is concerned.

DISCUSSION QUESTIONS

1. How is age constructed in the educational setting?
2. What is the juvenile court's authority in the educational setting?
3. What is the significance of historical cases in educational settings?
4. Explain and describe the legal rights of juveniles over time.

REFERENCES

Aikens, N. L., & Barbarin, O. (2008). Socioeconomic differences in reading trajectories: The contribution of family, neighborhood, and school contexts. *Journal of Educational Psychology, 100*(2), 235–251.

Bartollas, C., & Miller, J. S. (2010). *Juvenile justice in America.* Upper Saddle River, NJ: Pearson.

Beger, R. R. (2002). Expansion of police power in public schools and the vanishing rights of students. *Social Justice: A Journal of Crime, Conflict & World Order, 29*(1), 119.

Bachman, J. G., Green, S., & Wirtanen, I. (1971). *Youth in transition: Dropping-out- problem or symptom?* (Vol. III). Ann Arbor, MI: Institute for Social Research.

Bradley, R. H., Corwyn, R. F., McAdoo, H. P., & García Coll, C. (2001). The home environments of children in the United States part I: Variations by age, ethnicity, and poverty status. *Child Development, 72*(6), 1844–1867.

Buckingham, J., Wheldall, K., & Beaman-Wheldall, R. (2013). Why poor children are more likely to become poor readers: The school years. *Australian Journal of Education, 57*(3), 190–213.

Cohen, A. K. (1955). *Delinquent boys: The culture of the gang.* New York, NY: Free Press.

Commonwealth v. Fisher, 62 A. 198 (Pa. 1905).

Curtis, G. B. (1976). The checkered career of Parens Patriae: The State as parent or tyrant? *DePaul Law Review, 25*(4), 895–915.

Elder, G. H. (1985). Perspective on the life-course. In G. H. Elder (Ed.). *Life-course dynamics: Trajectories and Transitions, 1968–1980.* Ithaca, NY: Cornell University Press.

Elder, G. H., & Rockwell, R. C. (2010). The ecology of human development relates patterns of development to. *SAGE Directions in Educational Psychology,* 25.

Elliott, D. S. (1978). Delinquency and school dropout. In L. D. Savitz & N. Johnston (Eds.), *Crime in society* (pp. 453–469). New York, NY: Wiley.

Elliott, D. S., & Voss, H. L. (1974). *Delinquency and Dropout.* Lexington, MA: Heath.

Elrod, P., & Ryder, R. S. (2011). *Juvenile justice: a social, historical, and legal perspective.* Sudbury, MA: Jones and Bartlett.

Empey, L. T., Stafford, M. C., & Hay, C. H. (1982). *American delinquency: Its meaning and construction.* Homewood, IL: Dorsey Press.

Ex parte Crouse, 4 Wharton 9 (Pa. 1839).

Farrington, D. P. (1986). Steppingstones to adult criminal careers. In D. Olweus, J. Block, & M. R. Yarrow (Eds.), *Development of Antisocial and Prosocial Behavior* (pp. 359–384). New York, NY: Academic Press.

Gottfredson, D. C. (1997). School-based crime prevention. In L. W. Sherman, D. C. Gottfredson, D. MacKenzie, J. Eck, P. Reuter, & S. Bushway (Eds.), *Preventing crime: What works, what doesn't, what's promising: A report to the United States Congress* (pp. 5.1–5.74). Washington, DC: U.S. Department of Justice.

Grisso, T. E., & Schwartz, R. G. (2000). *Youth on trial: A developmental perspective on juvenile justice.* Chicago, IL: University of Chicago Press.

In re Winship, 397 U.S. 358 (1970)

Kolodinsky, J., Cranwell, M., & Rowe, E. (2002). Bridging the generation gap across the digital divide: Teens teaching internet skills to senior citizens. *Journal of Extension,* 40.

Krisberg, B., & Austin, J. F. (1993). *Reinventing juvenile justice.* Newbury Park, California: SAGE Publications.

Lawrence, R., & Hemmens, C. (2008). *Juvenile justice: A text/reader.* Sage. National Center for Education Statistics (NCES). (n.d.). Home page. Retrieved from https://nces.ed.gov/

NCES. (n.d.). NCES blog. Retrieved from https://nces.ed.gov/blogs/nces/2018/01/08/default

People ex rel. O'Connell v. Turner, 55 Ill. 280 (Ill. 1870).

Platt, A. M. (1977). *Child savers.* Chicago, IL: University of Chicago Press.

Sanborn, J. B., & Salerno, A. W. (2005). *The juvenile justice system: Law and process.* Los Angeles, CA: Roxbury Publishing Company.

U.S. Census Bureau. (2019, May 23). Which states spend the most money on their students? Retrieved from https://www.census.gov/library/stories/2018/06/school-spending.html

Waegel, W. B. (1989). *Delinquency and juvenile control: A sociological perspective.* Englewood Cliffs, NJ: Prentice Hall.

Weisner, T. S. (1984). Ecocultural niches of middle childhood: A cross-cultural perspective. In W. S. Collins (Ed.), *Development during middle childhood. The years from six to twelve* (pp. 335–369). Washington, DC: National Academy Press.

Figure Credit

Fig. 1.1: Source: https://www.loc.gov/item/2018675655/.

CHAPTER TWO

Poverty and Education Achievement

O. Oko Elechi

READING OBJECTIVES

- Understand the sources of poverty in society.
- Discuss how poverty affects readiness for school.
- Understand how poverty affects educational attainment.
- Examine strategies for reversing the effects of poverty on education.
- Understand other environmental factors that contribute to poor academic performance.
- Understand how poverty contributes to students' emotional and behavioral problems.
- Understand the challenges teachers face when dealing with poverty's effect on education.

OVERVIEW

Education is widely believed in America to be the gateway to economic well-being and a social equalizer. However, poverty remains a persistent problem in America and has a negative effect on behavior and academic performance. Poverty alienates people from society and makes it difficult for those caught in its web to control the events in their lives. Who and what we become as adults has a lot to do with our childhood experiences. In the United States, for example, your family income determines to a great extent the quality of education you will get, the neighborhood you live in, the nutritious meals you can have, your social contacts, and, therefore, your formative experiences. Family income, more than any other factor, has implications for an individual's life chances and well-being. Childhood poverty, therefore, has the potential to limit an individual's development and life chances and well-being. This is because individuals' family backgrounds determine their educational and career opportunities and inform their self-identity and esteem. Poverty and its consequent social inequality in America remain a major social challenge. The nation needs to start taking seriously the effect that poverty has on educational achievements; otherwise, America will lose its global scientific and technological advantage. As Tavernise (2012, p. 4) observed, "We have moved from a society in the 1950s and 1960s, in which race was more consequential than family income, to one today in which family income appears more determinative of educational success than race," as cited in Coley and Baker (2013).

However, it is imperative to point out that poverty, like all social and economic performances, does not happen in a vacuum, and it is not evenly distributed in America. Some subgroups are more affected by poverty than others. For example, African Americans, Hispanic Americans, and single mothers are poorer than the general public and constitute 21%, 18%, and 26% of the poor in society, respectively. In addition, 25% of adults with disabilities live in poverty.

It is important to note that poverty is as much an American problem as it is a big issue for the poor, as Royce (2015) stated. Again, poverty cannot just be explained away on the poor lacking hard-work, diligence, and self-advancing attitudes and habits. As Gorski (2013, p. 44) rightly pointed out, poverty is "tied to all sorts of other identities and forms of discrimination, including gender and sexism, race and racism, and even disability and ableism." Furthermore, certain structural and cultural changes are needed for poverty reduction. As Royce (2015, p. 65) pointed out, we need as a society to institute a "moral economy" that emphasizes national, rather than self, interest and the political and economic systems that promote the "principles of equity, fairness, and equality of opportunity." Royce further argued that people are poor because they lack the opportunities and the relevant resources essential for human development. Other factors that contribute to the high poverty rate in America today, according to Royce (2015, p. 54), include "the loss of jobs in the manufacturing sector, the growth of low-wage service industries, the accelerated pace of globalization and outsourcing, the decline of trade unions, the erosion in the real value of the minimum wage, and the surge of inequality."

According to the most recent report from the Federal Safety Net (2018), the U.S. poverty rate dropped to 12.3% in 2017. It was 12.7% in 2016. This is a 0.4 percentage point decline. It is also a 2.5 percentage drop in poverty from the 2014 poverty rate of 14.8% according to Fontenot, Semega, and Kollar (2018). The poverty rate for adults aged 18 to 64 also declined by 0.4 percentage points from 11.6% to 11.2%. For the 18-and-under category, the poverty rate remained unchanged at 18%. The poverty rate for the 65 and over category remained the same as in 2016 at 9.2%. ChildFund International (2013) further reported that about one in five children in America lives in poverty. For single-mother households, about 26% of them live in poverty, which is one out of three households headed by single mothers. On the other hand, "only 12 percent of poor children are raised in two-parent families, compared to 60 percent of all children," note Coley and Baker (2013, p. 4). The Federal Safety Net, in its September 2018 report, stated that 17.5% of American children live in poverty. That means that one out of five American children lives in poverty. The Federal Safety Net (2018) report stated that 39.7 million Americans live in poverty and that 9.3% of American families live below the poverty line. Families headed by a single mother were 5 times more likely to be in poverty according to this report. There are 15.4 million families in America headed by single mothers, which represents a whopping 51% of all the families that live below the official poverty line.

About 30% of children who are raised in poverty fail to complete high school. People who do not achieve their high school diploma by age 20, according to the study, are 7 times more likely to live in poverty between the ages of 25 and 30. Poverty affects the educational attainment and health conditions of people. Beard (2016), states that about 14% of American households were food insecure in 2014. Children account for about 12.8% of the American populace living below the poverty line. Poverty limits students' access to education and other economic opportunities. Poverty affects educational attainment in several ways. Children who live in poverty, for example, are more likely to be absent from school or drop out of school entirely because they may need to work to supplement family earnings or stay home to provide needed care for a family member. The school dropout rate among 16- to 24-year-old students who live in poverty is 7 times greater than that of students from families with higher incomes. That there is a strong link between poverty and poor educational achievement is irrefutable, but what is more worrisome is that about 31% of young adults who failed to complete high school were more likely to live in poverty. On the other hand, only about 24% of young adults who have high school diplomas are in poverty. Moreover, the poor are alienated from mainstream society, and, as Kenneth Clark (1965) observed, "human beings who live apart from the rest of society, who do not share in society's affluence, and who are not respected or granted the ordinary dignities and courtesy accorded to others will eventually begin to doubt their own worth," as cited in Dye and Harrison (2005, p. 297).

It goes without saying that children who live in poverty are not prepared for embarking on primary education. As a matter of fact, children living in poverty are 1.3 times more likely to suffer from other malaise, such as learning disabilities or other developmental delays, than those who do not live in poverty. As a matter of fact, children living in poverty are also more likely to suffer from other emotional and behavioral problems by age 5 that militate against their educational performance. Partly accounting for students' emotional and other behavioral problems are their mothers' psychological well-being and their parents' educational achievement. Poverty accounts for why African Americans, Hispanics, and other low-income students are generally 2 years behind that of other students not living in poverty. This educational disadvantage continues throughout their educational careers such that students living in poverty are likely to fall behind their peers who are not living in poverty by 4 years by the time they reach the 12th grade. Poverty plagues the educational careers of students. For example, about 30 percent of students in poverty do not complete high school according to Operation Warm (2018). They also argued that poverty affects a child in various ways that militate against their educational development. Poverty, according to them, affects a child's brain development and self-confidence. It can also cause heart disease and toxic stress. Children in poverty are likely to feel that they lack the power to control their circumstances thereby contributing to their being in a state of learned helplessness.

UNDERSTANDING THE CONCEPT OF POVERTY

There is no general agreement on what constitutes poverty. Our understanding of who is poor changes from place to place and from time to time. A family is considered living below the poverty line when the members' combined total income falls below a certain defined income threshold. In the United States, for example, a family of four making an annual income below $25,750 in 2017 was considered poor. This is the minimum amount that the United States, through its cost of living estimates, believes a family of four can subsist on in a year. On the other hand, the World Bank in 2015 determined that an individual making less than $1.90 a day in the developing world is living below the international poverty line. Simply put, someone who lacks the money to purchase certain basic needs or the resources to acquire socially acceptable material possessions is considered poor. Children living in poverty typically experience hunger and homelessness, and they often die from preventable and treatable diseases. Moreover, the educational achievement of children living in poverty lags behind students from affluent homes. This is often the lot of the majority of children in the developing world. Poverty, which is a lack of material resources, affects the social, economic, and political well-being of the individual too. As Books (2004, p. 5) aptly observed, children living in poverty "suffer hunger and homelessness, untreated sickness and chronic conditions such as asthma, ear infections, and tooth decay; lead poisoning and other forms of environmental pollution; and a sometimes debilitating level of distress created by crowded, run-down living spaces, family incomes that fall short of family needs, and ongoing threats of street violence and family dissolution."

Books also observed that children living in poverty are more likely to attend public schools that lack basic amenities because of underfunding. The buildings in the schools where predominantly poor children attend are often dilapidated and in a state of disrepair. Poverty has significant effects on the mind, body, and soul of a child in complex ways. The life span of the average poor person is often shorter than that of the more affluent members of the community. This is because the poor often have limited access to good medical care. The infant mortality rate among the poor is often much higher than that of the general public. Poor children are also more likely to live in one-parent homes.

There are many perspectives on why people are poor, especially in a rich country like the United States with its abundant resources and opportunities. We will briefly review two perspectives that try to explain poverty in society—namely, the individual and structural perspectives. The individual perspective locates the problem of poverty on the individual according to Royce (2015). In the individual perspective, people are poor because of their own failings. On the other hand, the structural perspective argues that people are poor in society because of the failings of society; in other words, it is more a structural rather than an individual failing. The individualistic perspective, according to Royce (2015), claims that people are poor because they hold or exhibit the wrong values and attitudes that are not supportive of progress. The structural perspective counters this argument by suggesting that poverty is a reflection of the effects of the workings of the economic, political, cultural, and social institutions of society.

The individualistic perspective further argues that the poor are poor because of their own failure to take advantage of the opportunities that are available to them. The structural perspective, on the other hand, argues that poverty is the failure of the economic and political systems of society to provide sufficient opportunities or enabling environments for some of its citizens.

The individualistic perspective blames poverty on the individual's wrong choices or decisions. In contrast, the structural perspective insists that poverty results more from the inability of the economic and political systems to provide options for every person, thereby creating winners and losers. Furthermore, the individualistic perspective argues that the obstacles to economic achievement are found within the individual's drive, and so when that is lacking, an individual cannot achieve much. The structural perspective disagrees, insisting that the obstacles to achievement are located within the larger economic and political environments. The poor, according to the individualistic perspective, are more likely lazy, have no work skills, and lack relevant education. The structural perspective lays the blame of poverty, instead, on the low-paying, lousy, dead-end jobs that the economic system provides, according to Royce (2015).

POVERTY AND EDUCATION

Poverty affects a child's education in several ways. There is evidence to support the contention that poverty affects a child's ability to succeed in his or her educational pursuits. Poverty contributes in significant ways to a child's social, emotional, and behavioral problems. Poverty affects a person's health and mental well-being. Poorer people live shorter lives because of their impoverishment. Michael Abramowitz and Lori Montgomery in their Washington Post article of February 1, 2007, titled "Bush Addresses Income Inequality," noted, "Poorer people die younger and are sicker than rich people." There is considerable evidence to support the thinking that poverty undermines a child's well-being and is one of the greatest threats to success in public schools. Adults who grew up in poverty-stricken homes often have low earning power. As a result, they pay lower taxes and are more likely to exhibit deviant behaviors. They also experience health conditions that undercut the nation's economy in several ways. Coley and Baker (2013), citing Holzer, Schanzenback, Duncan, and Ludwig (2007), noted that the estimated annual cost to the U.S. economy associated with child poverty is $500 billion, which is about 4% of the gross domestic product. In other words, childhood poverty is detrimental to individuals, families, and the nation in myriad ways, including affecting their social and economic development and well-being.

Family income, according to relevant studies, has a direct effect on students' performance on standardized tests. For example, "the gap in standardized test scores between affluent and low-income students had grown by about 40 percent since the 1960s and is now double the testing gap between Blacks and Whites," according to Tavernise (2012, p. 4), as cited by Coley and Baker (2013, p. 9). The report further states that the achievement gap on standardized tests between students from low-income households and the scores by students from high-income households is significant. The report notes that there is a strong correlation between poverty and cognitive skills. Underscoring this assertion is data from the Early Childhood Longitudinal Study, Birth Cohorts, which showed that about 67% of toddlers from families whose incomes were above the poverty line were proficient in expressive vocabulary as opposed to the 55% of toddlers from poverty-stricken families whose cognitive skills were at the same level. Lareau (2018) further observes that the quality of parenting a child receives has a lot to do with socio-economic class of his or her family. In other words, the socio-economic class of the family has implications for the quality of parenting and academic development of the child. Upper class parents, for example, are more likely to cultivate the talents and skills of their children and tailor their education accordingly. On the other hand, working class parents have less influence over the direction of the educational development of their children.

The preschoolers' test scores mirrored those of the toddlers. For example, the NCES in 2009 showed that 72% of 4-year-olds with family incomes above the poverty line revealed proficiency in identifying numbers and shapes as opposed to only 45% of 4-year-olds from families whose incomes were below the poverty line. A similar study undertaken by the NCES in 2011 revealed through the National Assessment of Educational Progress that fourth graders who were eligible for free lunch in school determined through family income scored 29 points lower on academic proficiency tests than students from households who did not qualify for school free lunch because their families' incomes were above the poverty line, according to Coley and Baker (2013). The outcome of a similar academic assessment carried out on eighth graders revealed the same pattern.

Other studies also show a correlation between family income and SAT test scores. According to the data from the College Board (2012), high school seniors from high-income families scored at least 100 points more than their counterparts from families whose incomes fell below the poverty line, as noted by Coley and Baker (2013). The Coley and Baker report under review indicated that family income levels also determine who goes to and completes college. They cited the University of Michigan study that analyzed data from the U.S. Census titled the Longitudinal Survey of Youth between 1979 and 1997. The study was undertaken to understand the differences in educational performance between students born in the early 1960s and those born in the early 1980s. According to Bailey and Dynarski (2011), students from homes whose incomes were above the poverty line gained 18 percentage points in college completion rates over students from households whose incomes fell below the poverty line, as cited in Coley and Baker (2013, p. 10).

Royce (2015) observed that about 70% of students who attend elite universities often come from the top economic quartile as opposed to the 3% of students who come from the bottom quartile. One explanation for this is that poorer students have all the cards stacked against them. Poorer students' backgrounds have not prepared them well enough to compete with students from affluent homes on the SAT test. Poorer students are also less likely to attend 4-year colleges, especially elite colleges. Elite institutions target private schools and public schools in rich neighborhoods that often have school counselors who have strong connections to recruitment officers from elite schools. Furthermore, students from wealthy backgrounds are more likely to register for expensive SAT preparatory classes. They are also coached on how to write resumes, prepare for interviews, and apply for financial assistance that may be available. Their parents may also be donors to the endowments of the elite institutions, which makes it possible that their children's applications will receive special consideration that is not possible for students born into poverty.

Another challenge for students from poorer homes is the cost of a college education. College education costs, according to Royce (2015), have increased steadily over the years at the same time that wages have stagnated and financial aid to students has been reduced, barely covering tuition and board. Suzanne Mettler, according to Royce (2015, p. 215), states that "the cost of attending a four-year public university increased from 6 to 9 % of family income for those in the wealthiest quintile and from 42 to 114 % for those in the poorest quintile."

Another advantage that students from affluent families have is that they attend private schools. Private schools have notable advantages over public schools. Private schools, according to the NCES published by Lindenberger (2019), have lower student-to-teacher ratios than public schools, which means that students get better attention than they would have received in public schools. The student-to-teacher ratio in private schools is 12:2 whereas the ratio in public schools is 16:1, according to the report. Furthermore, private schools, according to the Lindenberger report, emphasize preparing their students for college by offering different relevant advanced placement courses. According to the report, private school students outperform students from public schools on ACT tests by 3:1 points. The Lindenberger (2019, p. 3) report further states that "a comparison of mathematics tests showed private schools scored 18 points higher for eighth graders and 8 points higher for fourth graders. Reading had the same results with the private schools outscoring their public counterparts by 18 points in eighth grade and 15 points in fourth grade." Public schools do not charge tuition, whereas private schools charge between $6,890 to around $21,510 annually on average. Very few students from families with incomes lower than the poverty line can afford to attend private schools.

The learning environment in private schools seems more supportive of students' efforts. Teachers in private schools, for one, are more motivated and held to a higher standard, as the proprietors seek to impress the students who are more or less customers who must be satisfied with the services they receive to keep coming. The fee-paying parents are often highly educated and from affluent economic backgrounds, and so they can dictate to the schools what they want for their children's development and academic interests. As Wysong, Perrucci, and Wright (2014, p. 228) have observed, "One of the main concerns of the privileged class is to protect their advantage and to transmit it to their children." In this sense, it is understandable why the affluent members of society prefer private to public schools. For example, Dynarski, according to the Lindenberger report, observed that private schools create a more conducive peer environment. "Part of the reason for this phenomenon is the fact that private schools can screen who they allow in, and can tailor their offerings to the type of child they want coming through their doors" (Lindenberger, 2019, p. 3). Educating to meet the needs of the child, whether college bound or not, is what is called tracking. Wysong, Perrucci, and Wright (2014, p. 220) further argued that "tracking seems to be a very progressive idea, permitting teachers to tailor instruction to the ability level of their students. A good fit between a student's ability and the level of instruction is believed to maximize the effectiveness and efficiency of the instructional process."

The foregoing issues, unfortunately, undercut the ability of educational programs to level the playing field and create enabling and equitable environments for everyone. The funding formula for education in the country creates winners and losers. Schools in the poor neighborhoods that students from families living below the poverty line typically attend are poorly funded and often have the largest classes and the lowest paid teachers. Students attending schools in poor neighborhoods also experience violence, such as bullying. The buildings where poor students attend school are more likely to be poorly maintained and lack basic facilities.

CHILDHOOD POVERTY IN AMERICA

The Education Testing Service (ETS), in one of its publications, notes that one out of every five children in the United States lives in poverty. Moreover, child poverty is concentrated more in some subgroups than in others. For example, children in African American and Hispanic households are more likely to live in poverty than children from Caucasian households, as shown in Table 2.1. What is more worrying is that American children rank the second highest in poverty among the world's richest countries, despite the fact that America is the richest country in the world. The fact that some ethnic groups, especially minorities, suffer from the problem of childhood poverty more than others is a cause for concern. That also has implications for racial relationships and harmony in the country, because it produces differential economic outcomes for the different ethnic groups in the country.

TABLE 2.1   *Overview of Childhood Poverty and Disadvantage in the United States*

Adults not working	31%
Single moms	26%
Adults with a disability	25%
Adults without a high school diploma	25%
Black Americans	21%
Foreign born noncitizens	19%
Hispanic Americans	18%
All children	18%
Single dads	12%
Seniors	9%
Married couples	5%
Adults with a college degree or higher	5%
Full-time working adults	2%

Sources: U.S Poverty Statistics from the Federal Safety Net report of September 2018 (http://federalsafe-tynet.com/us-poverty-statistics.html).

HOW POVERTY AFFECTS EDUCATION AND ADULT OUTCOMES

The following describes how poverty negatively affects education and learning:

1. **Poor nutrition.** A child living in poverty can hardly afford to eat a nutritious or balanced diet. Children raised in poor neighborhoods are likely to live off fast food and prepackaged foods rather than fresh and healthier foods that are more expensive. Poor parents are also often working more than one job

and, therefore, lack the time to prepare a healthy meal for their children. Poor diet affects a child's learning ability and overall well-being. The cognitive disadvantage that poverty engenders could be caused by other environmental factors that are beyond the control of individuals, such as environmental toxins, exposure to violence, and prenatal drug use.

2. **Impaired health.** Poverty affects the quality of food children consume. Children growing up in poverty do not have access to well-balanced meals on a regular basis. And because they do not eat nutritious food, they are, therefore, susceptible to different kinds of illnesses, such as asthma and ear infections. Children who suffer from these illnesses without adequate medical treatment are more likely to miss school or other school activities. This can affect their learning and even lead to them dropping out of school for some.

3. **Limited physical activity.** Children who grow up poor often reside in poverty-stricken neighborhoods that lack resources, such as after-school academic and physical enrichment programs. This may affect their ability to focus and concentrate on their schoolwork.

4. **Stress.** Children living in poverty often experience unstable and negative environmental conditions that affect their behaviors in varied ways. This can contribute to aggressive and inappropriate behaviors with other students and authority figures. Furthermore, they may be unable to build healthy relationships with their peers and school administrators, which can affect their learning. Poor students encounter stress in many ways, such as wearing dirty clothes and tardiness, which brings them into conflict with school authorities.

5. **Verbal ability.** Children living in poverty have limited access to reading materials and fewer opportunities to engage in conversations that enhance their cognitive development like their peers from middle-class households. With a limited vocabulary, they are unable to learn and compete effectively. Educated parents know how to engage their children in conversations that stimulate creative responses that enhance their verbal development and self-confidence. Improved verbal skills make it easier for students to relate to their peers, teachers, and school administrators and to shore up their self-esteem and sense of agency.

TACKLING POVERTY'S EFFECT ON EDUCATION

Several factors, such as household income, household structure, parental education, and occupational status, have a significant effect on a child's self-concept, self-esteem, standards, and values. These factors consequently affect a child's skills and knowledge acquisition, school performance, and educational attainment. The government is capable of introducing policies that can ameliorate the effect of poverty and social inequality on education. Government policies can reduce childhood poverty, for example, and, therefore, its effect on education. Poverty and its consequent inequality impact both individual and national economies and well-being. Duncan and Magnuson (2011) reported from their study on income dynamics, as cited in Coley and Baker (2013), that there is a strong correlation between a family's income and a child's outcome as an adult. According to the study findings, children who grow up in a family whose income falls below the American official poverty line had 2 years less schooling than those whose family income was above the U.S. official poverty line.

Children growing up in poverty earned less than 50% in wages in their lifetimes than those who grew up in homes whose family income was above the official poverty line. Those growing up in poverty, according to this report, received $826 more in food stamps per year than their counterparts from wealthier homes. They were also more likely to suffer from poor health. Above all, males growing up in poverty were 2 times more likely than their counterparts from middle-class homes to be arrested for criminal behavior. In the same vein, females growing up in poverty were 5 times more likely to have a child out of wedlock than their counterparts from relatively richer homes. Duncan and Magnuson (2011) "suggested that a substantial portion of the simple correlation between childhood income and most adult outcomes can be accounted for by the negative conditions associated with birth into a low-income household," as cited in Coley and Baker (2013, p. 8).

The study under review, however, suggested that if the government can intervene effectively, education has the potential to mitigate the negative effects of poverty on children and social inequality. A good education can equip children with the relevant knowledge and skills needed to lead a productive and successful life in modern society. A good and functional education is perhaps the first step in helping an individual get out of poverty. DuBois (2001, p. 133) insisted that children living in poverty are not doomed to failure, provided that relevant and thoughtful policies are put in place by both local and national government agencies. DuBois said children can be taught resilience and positive self-concept and suggested that "individual factors identified as promoting resilience are several interrelated aspects of the self, including a strong positive self-concept or sense of self-efficiency, personal values and aspirations oriented toward success in important life domains, such as school, and high self-esteem." (DuBois, 2001, p. 133)

Poverty signifies a lack of resources by parents to provide for their children. The government can provide additional resources to cushion the negative effects of poverty on the family. Poverty amelioration programs, such as direct subsidy, social services, and tax benefits, can be extended to needy families. Both governmental and nongovernmental agencies can advocate for and secure the necessary support for schools that lack resources to enhance equity of academic outcomes. Other governmental and nongovernmental advocacy and support groups can provide the necessary intervention programs that advance academic, social, and community development and well-being. It may be possible to allow schools in poor neighborhoods to operate longer school days and after-school programs. Increasing school funding, in this case, can help reduce the gap between poor children and middle-class students in their academic performance. One way that the additional funding can be used is by offering free meals to students during school time and holidays to address the holiday hunger of schoolchildren from poorer households.

Government funding can also be used to provide school uniforms and relevant technological materials that make teaching and learning more engaging and enhance personal self-esteem. Educators can be trained and sensitized to understand the needs of students in high-poverty schools to make additional efforts to raise expectations for higher academic performance.

Parents of students in high-poverty schools can also be encouraged to undertake training that enhances their skills and knowledge. They can also engage in collective political action that gets the attention of political power brokers and leads to the equitable distribution of necessary funds and resources. The decentralization of power and resources can only be achieved through political action and campaigns. Poverty is created by governmental policies and actions and can also be resolved through alternative policies. One policy that can achieve this objective is focused investments that address the effect of poverty on education. Unequal school funding can also create unequal skills, knowledge, and student experiences. Knowledge and skills are not created equal; some knowledge and skills can raise the social consciousness of students and enhance their sense of agency and political participation. With more money, schools can hire better qualified teachers and school administrators, purchase up-to-date equipment, hire more qualified school counselors, and provide extracurricular activities. As Royce (2015, p. 217) rightly observed, "Creating more equal schools would be a step in the right direction. Ultimately, however, only by creating a more equal society can the educational achievement gap between the rich and the poor be narrowed."

DISCUSSION QUESTIONS

1. What are the sources of poverty in society?
2. How does poverty affect school readiness?
3. How does poverty affect educational attainment?
4. What strategies can be implemented to reverse the effects of poverty on education?
5. What environmental factors contribute to poor academic performance?
6. How does poverty contribute to students' emotional and behavioral problems?
7. What are the challenges teachers face when dealing with poverty's effect on education?

REFERENCES

Abrahmowitz, M. and Montogomery, L. (2007) "Bush Addresses Income Inequality" (http://www.washingtonpost.com/wp-dyn/content/article/2007/01/31/AR2007013100879_pf.html) retrieved on 11/3/2019)

Books, S. (2004). *Poverty and schooling in the U.S.: Contexts and consequences.* Mahwah, NJ: Lawrence Erlbaum Associates.

Biddle, B. J. (2001). *Poverty, ethnicity, and achievement in American schools in social class, poverty, and education: Policy and practice.* New York, NY: Routledge Falmer.

ChildFund International. (2013). The effects of poverty on education in the United States: Statistics on poverty and education in the United States. Retrieved from https://www.childfund.org/Content/NewsDetail/2147489206/.

Clark, K. B. (1965). *Dark Ghetto: Dilemmas of Social Power.* New York: Harper & Row.

Coley, R. J., & Baker, B. (2013). *Poverty and education: Finding the way forward.* Princeton, NJ: Educational Testing Service.

DuBois, D. L. (2001). *Family disadvantage, the self, and academic achievement in American schools in social class, poverty, and education: Policy and practice.* New York, NY: Routledge Falmer.

Duncan, G.J. and Magnuson, K. (2011). Early Childhood Poverty. https://inequality.stanford.edu/sites/default/files/media/_media/pdf/pathways/winter_2011/PathwaysWinter11_Duncan.pdf

Dye, T. R., & Harrison, B. C. (2005). *Power and society: An introduction to the social sciences* (10th ed.). Belmont, CA: Thomson Wadsworth.

Dynarski, M. (2014). https://www.brookings.edu/research/public-or-private-school-it-shouldnt-matter.

Federal Safety Net (2018). U.S. poverty statistics. Retrieved from http://federalsafetynet.com/us-poverty-statistics.html

Fontenot, K., Semega, J., & Kollar, M. (2018). Income and poverty in the United States: 2017. Retrieved from https://www.census.gov/library/publications/2018/demo/p60-263.html

Gorski, P. C. (2013). *Reaching and teaching students in poverty: Strategies for erasing the opportunity gap.* New York, NY: Teachers College Press.

Holyfield, L. (2002). *Moving up and out: Poverty, education, and the single parent family.* Philadelphia, PA: Temple University Press.

Lareau, A. (2018). Unequal childhoods: Class, race, and family life. In K. McGann (Ed.), *Sage readings for introductory sociology.* Los Angeles, CA: Sage.

Lindenberger, H. (2019, June 26). Public school vs. private school: Teachers. Retrieved from https://www.yahoo.com/lifestyle/private-school-vs-public-school-182646593.html

Mettler, S. (2014). "College: The Great Unleveler," New York Times of March 2, 2014.

National Centre for Educational Statistics (NCES) (2011). (https://nces.ed.gov/) retrieved on 10/28/2019.

Operation Warm (2018). Long-term Impacts of Poverty on Children: Health & Education. (https://www.operationwarm.org/blog/long-term-impacts-of-poverty-on-children-health-Education) retrieved on 10/28/2019.

Royce, E. (2015). *Poverty and power: The problem of structural inequality* (2nd ed.). New York, NY: Rowman and Littlefield.

Tavernise, S. (2002). "Education Gap Grows Between Rich and Poor, Studies Say." New York Times, February 9, 2012.

West, A. (2007). Poverty and educational achievement: Why do children from low-income families tend to do less well at school? *The Policy Press, Benefits,15*(3, 2007), 283–297.

Wysong, E., Perrucci, R., & Wright, D. (2014). *The new class society: Goodbye American dream?* (4th ed.). New York, NY: Rowman & Littlefield Publishers, Inc.

CHAPTER THREE

The School-to-Prison Pipeline

J. Renee Trombley

READING OBJECTIVES

- Understand how themes of punishment affect education.
- Discuss the connection between the school-to-prison pipeline and the prison industrial complex.
- Understand how the war on drugs affected educational settings.
- Examine strategies for dismantling the school-to-prison pipeline.
- Understand how zero-tolerance policies in schools result in exclusionary discipline policies.
- Understand how gun-free schools contribute to the school-to-prison pipeline.

OVERVIEW

Over the last few decades, overarching themes of punishment and deterrence have dominated the policies and practices within the United States' criminal and juvenile justice systems. This ideology has laid the foundation for detrimental effects and consequences, particularly for our youth. This can be seen in the overwhelmingly vast cases of unethical treatment of youth who, through their participation in an educational system designed to serve them, have been subjected to harsh and discriminatory treatment and marginalized and penalized through zero-tolerance policies, exclusionary practices, and proliferation of policing in schools, as well as through a focus on high-stakes testing (Curtis, 2014; McCarter, 2016). The impacts of these policies are now evident.

These youth are being pushed out of schools, both directly and indirectly, and into the criminal justice system through a funnel created by organizational and administrative policies and procedures, as well as discriminatory treatment through unjust and unethical practices. Harsh school discipline and exclusionary policies directly lead students to interactions with the police and courts, while indirectly these policies lead to reductions in educational performance and decreased connections in schools, resulting in increases in delinquency and risk of incarceration (Mizel et al., 2016). Overwhelmingly, these burdens have been placed on African American and Hispanic youth, disabled youth, and other special populations. These youth come in direct line of fire when facing harsh disciplinary action for relatively minor incidents and infractions, creating a clear path to the criminal justice system and, eventually, prison.

SCHOOL-TO-PRISON PIPELINE

The school-to-prison pipeline is an established metaphor, often used to vividly describe the funneling of students from America's school system into the criminal justice system. According to McGrew (2016), the growth of this term developed shortly after a 2003 conference held at Northeastern University entitled Reconstructing the School-to-Prison Pipeline: Charting Intervention Strategies of Prevention and Support for Minority Children. Several papers published from this conference served to proliferate the conversation through their examination of the effect of a decade of get-tough policies and practices in schools that were implemented during an era defined by the growth of mass incarceration in the criminal justice system in America.

Research began consistently linking concepts of the school-to-prison pipeline with the prison industrial complex (McGrew, 2016), and, overwhelmingly, the conclusion is that this pipeline, both directly and indirectly, feeds students into the criminal justice system (Heitzeg, 2009; Ruiz, 2017). The fact that criminal justice is a big business in the United States is indisputable. The United States currently has more people locked up in prison per capita than any other democratic nation in the world (Sentencing Project/Facts, n.d.). Over the last few decades, the rate of incarceration in America skyrocketed. Between 1980 and 2015, the number of people incarcerated in the United States climbed from around 500,000 to more than 2.2 million, and in 2016, 1 in every 37 adults in this country was under some form of correctional supervision (National Association for the Advancement of Colored People, n.d.).

Research shows specific factors supporting the school-to-prison pipeline. The development of zero-tolerance policies almost two decades ago has led to the over-incarceration of youth through zero-tolerance policies for drug laws and gun laws. Yet, in reality these policies have actually been applied in the most menial of cases, and this has had harmful effects on thousands of children who have been pushed out of schools, increasing the harm and oppression experienced by students already coming from marginalized populations (Gage et al., 2013). These policies provide overly punitive penalties that hurt students who are already struggling at school and may be further behind than their peers, including youth who struggle with mental illness and learning disabilities (Monterastelli, 2016). Overwhelmingly, the students most impacted by these policies are African American and Latino youth, as well as youth from other already marginalized populations, including those in the LGBTQ community (McNeal, 2016; Eitle & Eitle; 2004; Snapp et al.). While the overall impacts of zero-tolerance policies have been considerably harmful for them, some lawmakers continue to enhance policies allowing for the criminalization of our youth (Moyer, 2017).

ZERO-TOLERANCE POLICIES AND IMPLICATIONS FOR THE PIPELINE

One of the glaring attributes of the school-to-prison pipeline is the way zero-tolerance policies have shaped the culture in our educational institutions. Zero-tolerance policies can be defined as including any legislation and/or regulation that requires a specific and mandatory response to certain infractions, regardless of any additional facts in the case. Castillo (2014, p. 44), noted,

> Zero-tolerance policies are the most severe forms of school discipline today. These policies strip school administrators of discretion and impose predetermined penalties for a given infraction, without consideration of mitigating circumstances or unique situations that may have led to the incident.

Research shows that the term "zero-tolerance" originated first in relation to conversations about drug enforcement policies and federal drug seizures that were taking place during the get-tough era on crime (Novak, 2018). During the 1980s, and under the Reagan administration, the war on drugs flourished and quickly became a subject of concern among local education agencies across the country that began to use the term "zero tolerance" in relation to policies within school legislation that mandated specific responses for student violations (McNeal, 2016). One such change happened in 1986 with the introduction of federal legislation amending the Title 21 U.S.C. Controlled Substances Act through SS860, requiring mandatory minimum penalties for the distribution or manufacturing of any controlled substance in or near any school, college, university, or other academic institution as identified through the local education agencies (DEA Diversion Control Division, n. d.). Establishing drug-free school zones was meant to protect youth from dangerous criminals but was actually one of the first pieces of legislation that began enabling the overcriminalization of students in our educational institutions.

Two years later, in 1988, the National Coalition for Drug-Free Schools was created using members from several groups, including the National School Board Association, the National Association of Elementary School Principals, the National Association of Secondary School Principals, the National School Safety Center, the National Association of State Alcohol and Drug Abuse Directors, the National Conference of

State Legislatures, the National Council of Juvenile and Family Court Judges, and the Chiefs of Police National Drug Task Force, as well as several other organizations (National Criminal Justice Reference Service, n. d.). Together, they developed an implementation manual to support the drug-free school zone initiative. The purpose of this manual was to educate and provide guidance for community task forces in establishing and promoting drug-free school zones across the states.

Zero-tolerance policies related to alcohol, tobacco, and drug violations on school grounds from elementary schools to college campuses quickly grew. Infractions occurring off-campus while attending a school-related event could also incur these preset mandatory penalties. This get-tough approach quickly became the norm, and by 1998, 90% of schools had some form of zero-tolerance policies related to alcohol, tobacco, and drug infractions (Lynch, Gainey, & Chappell, 2016). But zero-tolerance policies were continuing to expand, most specifically through legislation focusing on the possession of weapons.

Drug-Free Schools

Research attributes a large portion of this growth to the politics of the drug war. In 1971, Nixon officially declared the war on drugs, but it was not until the early '80s that Americans began to feel the effects of the war on drugs through a rising incarceration rate (Public Broadcasting Station, n.d.). The revitalization of the war on drugs in the 1980s signaled the beginning of a get-tough approach in the criminal justice system. A rise in the level of incarceration rates in the United States began, and mass incarceration became a by-product of the conservative political agenda of the time.

Legislation supporting new mandatory minimum policies were introduced through the Anti-Drug Abuse Act of 1986, which also served to create severe racial disparities through sentencing guideline differences between crack cocaine and powder cocaine (Drug Policy Alliance, n.d.). Described as the "100-to-1" ratio, the Anti-Drug Abuse Act established mandatory minimums for amounts of crack cocaine that required at least 100 times of powder cocaine to trigger the same mandatory minimum sentence (United States Sentencing Commision, n. d.). These policies significantly increased racial disparities in the criminal justice system, and continued disparities in the rates of incarceration have been evident since this time. For instance, in 2014, there were 2.3 million African Americans in the correctional system, representing 34% of the total corrections population (National Association for the Advancement of Colored People, n.d.).

Average citizens who were overburdened with fear encouraged this trend of over-criminalization. They were afraid because, in so many ways, they were being told to be afraid. The image of the "superpredator" (Moriearty & Carson, 2015) had been introduced into the minds of Americans, and at the same time, they were bearing witness to the war on drugs during the crack cocaine era. Violence was everywhere according to the media, and the proof of this was witnessed every evening on the nightly news, as it was continually riddled with visions of inner-city violence spilling across the television screen. All of this played directly into the hands of a conservative agenda whose focus represented what had become known as the "get-tough era" in criminal justice reform. This directly tied into our characterizations of youth at the time, especially poor black males.

The idea of the "superpredator" first emerged in 1996, when a Princeton professor by the name of John DiIulio sent out a warning to the American public, describing juveniles who had no empathy, who were overly impulsive, and who were remorseless in their path to "murder, assault, rape, rob, burglarize, deal deadly drugs, join gun-toting gangs and create serious communal disorders" (Bennett, DiIulio, & Walters 1996, p. 27). This image bored into the American psyche, even though future research would prove these conceptions false and perceived threats unwarranted. However, the damage had been done, and one of the consequences of this propaganda was that it served to help fuel the racial disparities that have come to so clearly characterize our criminal and juvenile justice systems.

Between 2007 and 2009, a great recession hit the country, and the incarceration rate of prisoners nationwide slowly began to decline, in large part because of the outrageous costs of continuing to mass incarcerate American citizens. Yet there is still a long way to go. In 2019, millions of people, mostly black, brown, and poor, fill our prisons and jails. America continues to have the highest rate of incarceration compared with any other democratic nations in the world, and, most importantly, this has had a huge effect on youth in the United States.

As we continue to overincarcerate and consistently focus on punitive measures, we are only beginning to realize the total cost of the damage that this ideology has had on our children, particularly young black and Hispanic youth. In fact, the school-to-prison pipeline has already devastated the lives of countless youth through multiple exclusionary policies and practices that have stopped significant numbers of youth from completing their K–12 education experience. These practices have entangled youth within the juvenile justice system, and in doing so, they have increased their overall risk of becoming involved with the criminal justice system and facing future imprisonment.

Over the last few decades, the school-to-prison pipeline has grown extensively because of several different factors, but it is most closely associated with the proliferation of zero-tolerance policies, disparities in exclusionary discipline practices, and an overreliance on law enforcement in schools, as well as the use of high-stakes testing, focusing on standardized test scores, and other harmful practices (McCarter, 2016). The resulting influence has helped shape a culture within schools that actually resembles that of a correctional institution, equipped with police and law enforcement, officially known as school resource officers; metal detectors; locked doors to classrooms; and discussions on ways to further increase security in our education institutions. However, these practices have not earned overwhelming support in regard to their effectiveness in actually improving school safety, yet there is significant evidence of the damage and resulting harm that they have caused.

Gun-Free Schools

Zero-tolerance policies involving weapons were introduced into our schools through H.R.987—the Gun-Free Schools Act of 1993. This legislation requires that local educational agencies, as a condition of funding, mandate that any student caught bringing a gun, knife, or any other weapon must be expelled from school for at least one year (Gun Free School Act of 1993). In addition, this legislation authorized grants to local education agencies administered by the secretary of education to fund the training of security personnel and to make purchases for crime prevention equipment, including metal detectors in schools. This was all done in an effort to make schools safer. The Gun Free School Act would prove to have far reaching effects probably not envisioned by those who originally supported it.

Schools have had significant leeway in how they approach the development of specific policies following these directives. These policies were applied broadly and included language justifying the use of zero-tolerance for any kind/type of weapon, brought or possessed anywhere on school grounds or during any school-based event off school grounds. Like many policies and programs developed in an attempt to do good, these acts of legislation actually had harmful effects. The unintended and collateral consequences have been an instigating force in the proliferation of negative effects for youth, especially among youth coming from marginalized populations, especially those with multiple marginalized identities. Research finds these policies are directly implicated in the rise of the school-to-prison pipeline. Yet, Philip Mongan and Robert Walker (2012) find that research is lacking to provide any empirical support for the use of zero-tolerance policies provided by the Gun Free Schools legislation, arguing these policies are "theoretically unsound, empirically unsupported, and fall prey to several legal critiques."

Yet research shows that a large number of students who have been targeted through zero-tolerance policies were actually only culpable in very minor incidents. Some of these events included a student completing a writing assignment for a "scary" Halloween story, and while the student received an A for their work, they were referred to school officials, who contacted the police, and the child spent 6 days in jail before courts dismissed the case. Or the disturbing case of a 14-year-old disabled student who was accused of stealing $2.00 from another student, charged with strong-armed robbery, and held in an adult jail for 6 weeks before charges were dropped because of national attention of the case (Heitzeg, 2009). These cases could be considered minor compared to youth as young as 5 years old being handcuffed and arrested for having temper tantrums in the classroom or engaging in other very minor infractions.

These frivolous juvenile court referrals have served to criminalize youth misbehavior and resulted in helping to funnel students into the juvenile courts for trivial matters that could have been handled in the school between teachers and administrators by working with the child and the parents rather than involving law enforcement (Aull, 2012). In addition, comparative research finds that all is not created equal and that these policies are often applied discriminatingly, with minority youth and kids from other marginalized groups significantly likely to experience the harshest and severest penalties. These polices have been devastating for students and families that have found themselves entangled somewhere in the intersection of schools, zero-tolerance policies, and the juvenile justice system. Mallett (2016) provides a critical review of these policies and argues that school districts and the juvenile justice system in the United States were never meant to operate in a collaborative paradigm, yet this is exactly what is happening (2016).

School Resource Officers

School resource officers are essentially law enforcement officers who have been assigned by their employing police department to work in collaboration with one or more schools (NASRO, 2019). Examining the historical development of school resource officers shows cases of police operating in schools dating back as far as 80 years ago. Yet, more recently the number of school resource officers and the representation of a strong police presence in schools have begun to expand. It is not a coincidence that the proliferation of school resource officers occurred at relatively the same time that the federal government began endorsing broad based zero-tolerance policies while expanding the legal reach of schools through drug-free and gun-free legislation. The support of the federal government came through the allotment of federal dollars, distributed by the Department of Justice and the Department of Education, to support state school initiatives in enforcing zero-tolerance policies, including the authorization for funding for schools to invest in military equipment and tactical gear, as well as metal detectors and other security devices (Lynch, Gainey, & Chappell, 2016; Peak, 2015).

According to the National Association of School Resource Officers, currently there are anywhere from 14,000 – 20,000 SROs working in schools across the United States (NASRO, n.d.). There are large variations across the country with how many officers work in a given district. For instance, some schools may share one resource officer between several schools and yet in some larger districts hundreds of school resource officers may be employed, with several officers assigned to one school (Brown, 2006). For instance, in New York City, the public-school system's security division is large enough that if it was a police department it would be the 5th largest in the country (Peak, 2015). Combined with the number of school security guards, sworn law enforcement officers, and other school security employees currently working in schools, school security has become a big business in the United States, employing over 85,000 people in these positions (NCES, 2015).

Yet, the implementation of law enforcement officers in schools has not been well received by everyone. There have been many criticisms about the effectiveness of school resource officers to actually lower the rate of violence and crime that happens in schools. Critics argue that lack of empirical support for these policies should be considered as well as the extensive role that SROs play in the growth of the school-to-prison-pipeline. While teachers and parents are often advocates for advancing the educational opportunities of their students, the imposition of zero-tolerance policies and the presence of law enforcement in schools can be a destructive force preventing those possibilities (Abudu & Miles, 2017), Studies support the idea that there are several mitigating factors that impact the work of SROs on school campuses, including but not limited to the levels of social and economic disadvantage present in a school. Officers assigned to schools with higher levels of disadvantage were consistently more likely to spend a higher proportion of their working hours engaged in law enforcement activities and were less likely to be involved in education functions and campus events. These factors are considered as significant predictors for increasing exclusionary student discipline, student involvement with the juvenile justice system, and implicated in supporting the continuation of the school-to-prison-pipeline (Lynch, Gainey, & Chappell, 2016).

Research shows that schools reporting higher levels of economic disadvantage had significantly higher rates of arrests, especially for disorderly conduct. Disorderly conduct, like many other deviant behaviors, is a product of both situational and circumstantial factors that work both directly and indirectly to support the disproportionate rate of referrals for exclusionary discipline and arrests of minority students in schools (Theriot, 2009). One factor in how school resource officers see their work has to do with their level of education and training. Research finds significant differences in how officers approach their work with those having little or no training more likely to focus on law enforcement efforts, while those who reported seeking higher levels of specialized training were more likely to combine law enforcement duties with activities focused on supporting counseling interventions (Martinez-Prather, McKenna, & Bowman, 2016).

The relationship between decreased educational opportunities, exclusionary school discipline, and increasing risk for incarceration is well established (Cuellar & Markowitz, 2015; Skiba, 2013). Research shows that zero-tolerance policies with increases in law enforcement in schools have done little to improve the culture within our schools and classrooms. Instead, these policies continue to show negative and adverse outcomes, increasing students' risks of falling through the school-to-prison pipeline (Perry & Morris, 2014). Yet, studies continue to show the significance that education has across the life-course. In juveniles and young adults, education can provide a significant turning point, helping individuals escape and overcome experiences with crime and deviance (Blomberg, Bales, & Piquero, 2012). Yet, we know that zero-tolerance policies, harsh exclusionary discipline practices, and school-wide procedures continually funnel students into the juvenile justice system. In order to change this, we must begin by examining the use of exclusionary school practices.

Exclusionary School Practices

Zero-tolerance policies in schools have resulted in large numbers of students facing exclusionary discipline policies, through suspensions and expulsions, that directly remove students from classrooms and normal education opportunities for rule violations (Wilson, 2014). According to the Department of Education website, almost 50 million students were enrolled in public schools during the 2011–2012 school year. During that time 3.5 million students were assigned in-school suspensions, another 3.45 million students were given out-of-school suspensions, and an additional 130,000 students were officially expelled from school. In their efforts to control deviance in schools, government and school officials have instituted a variety of policies and practices that have continually gone overboard, resulting in the overcriminalization of youth in schools (Dennis, 2017). Those groups that have specifically been hit the hardest by these policies have primarily been youth from marginalized populations including Black and Latino youth, as well as youth with disabilities, and those who identify as lesbian, gay, bisexual, transgender, queer or questioning (LGBTQ) (Krezmien, Leone, Zablocki, & Wells, 2010).

Researchers argue over the importance of examining the influence of race in addressing discipline disparities in schools (Carter et al., 2017). Research shows that race is one of the most significant predictors of the use of harsh exclusionary practices in schools. Studies examining the impact of race continue to find evidence of disproportionate rates of exclusionary school discipline practices, including suspensions and expulsions (Wallace, Goodkind, Wallace, & Bachman, 2008). Overwhelmingly, research finds that African American youth are overrepresented in the use of exclusionary discipline. Welch and Payne (2010) found that schools that had higher levels of Black students were more likely to rely on zero-tolerance policies and punitive responses while also being less likely to engage students in rehabilitative or restorative responses. Black boys experience the highest levels of exclusionary discipline in schools (Mizel et al., 2016; Rich, 2016). Examining racial and gender differences in corporal punishment in schools finds that African American males were significantly more likely to be disciplined through these strategies (Gregory, 1995). Other studies support the idea that the culturally informed characteristics of Black girls often result in being labeled defiant and unruly, having a bad attitude and not being able to act with sophistication (White, 2018).

In addition to race, students who deal with learning and behavioral disabilities as well as those who have mental health issues are also more likely to face exclusionary discipline. These students are often labeled as problem children (Lavin, 2016), while at-risk youth are often labeled as troublemakers for their inability to meet expected demands in the class (Bowdich, 1993). This research shows that youth who perform poorly in classes often report being "pushed-out," and finds that 25% of students who had been labeled as dropping-out actually reported being "discharged coercively" (Bowditch, 1993). Additional research notes that teachers often label certain youth as "troublemakers," when in reality these students are often facing significant challenges at home and in their communities, yet these labels reinforce negative stigma around the youth and can divert and transform thoughts about a student needing services to that of a student who deserves punishment.

Teachers and Principals

Overwhelmingly, research points the finger at teachers and principals for their part in the proliferation of the school-to-prison pipeline. Several studies point to classrooms and the impact of teacher's decisions when referring students to the school principal's office for disciplinary action. Research has shown that while African American youth are significantly more likely to be referred to the office for disciplinary action, neither student behavior nor school-related factors could account for disparities that existed in the rates of referrals by teachers (Rocque, 2010). African American youth are scrutinized by teachers in the classroom more than their peers, more likely to be targeted for intense surveillance, and more likely to be sent to be discipled for infractions more subjective in nature, and referrals more often than not originated by the student's primary teacher (Skiba, Michael, Nardo, & Peterson, 2002). In one study researchers found that by 9th grade 48% of African American students had been suspended at least once (Arcia, 2007).

Studies on the roles teachers play in the school-to-prison pipeline find disparate treatment of Black students in the classroom and differences in the rates of referrals to the office for disciplinary action play a huge part in the number of students that are suspended and expelled each year. Even when similar offenses are examined research finds that Black students were significantly more likely to receive harsh punitive exclusionary discipline compared with White students, increasing risk for Black youths' susceptibility to involvement in the juvenile justice system (Nicholson-Crotty, Birchmeier, & Valentine, 2009). Overarching surveillance of Black youth in the classroom combined with a lack of training for teachers who work with diverse and underserved minority populations increase the implicit bias found in exclusionary discipline (Raible & Irizarry, 2010).

Yet, teachers surely don't carry all of the blame for the disproportionate use of exclusionary discipline among marginalized populations. Within the schools themselves, the biggest influence is the use of zero-tolerance policing by the principal of the school. These administrators share a significant portion of the responsibility for the culture that is created within their school (Skiba et al., 2014). Higher levels of disparities among class, race, and gender lines in a school is a reflection on the school principal's ability to support their students and faculty in developing rehabilitative, restorative, and socially just practices. However, seeking solutions to these problems is imperative. Youth who are pushed out of school and do not graduate are much more likely to be arrested, to be arrested more than once, and to face an increase in negative consequences across the life-course, including an increase in both mental and

physical health problems and reduced job opportunities and lifetime earning potential (Canadian Council on Learning, 2009; Cuellar, & Markowitz, 2015; Na, 2017).

Dismantling the School-to-Prison Pipeline
Research suggesting the need to dismantle the school-to-prison pipeline is significant.

In 2014, U.S. Secretary of Education Arne Duncan, during a speech at the release
of the Joint Department of Justice and the Department of Education, School Discipline Guidance Package, noted,

> The need to rethink and redesign school discipline practices is long overdue. Too
> many schools resort too quickly to exclusionary discipline, even for minor misbe-
> haviors. Exclusionary discipline is so common that in some cases, pre-K students
> as young as three- and four- years old are getting suspended … schools should
> remove students from the classroom as a last resort, and only for appropriately
> serious infractions, like endangering the safety of other students, teachers, or
> themselves. (U.S. Department of Education, n.d.).

Rich (2016) drew on the literature and offered several recommendations for dismantling the pipeline, such as the development of more holistic reforms to the current
criminal justice system; providing systematic changes to the national education
system, including the elimination of zero-tolerance policies while formally addressing the disparities in disciplinary actions across educational systems; and, finally,
acknowledging and addressing the failure of the "war on drugs" and the destructive
implications it has had for minority communities. These changes can support the
dismantling of the pipeline, but many argue that the classroom is the source of most
referrals and, therefore, training for teachers may be the most efficient and logical way
to attempt to change the number of students facing exclusionary discipline each year.

Research shows that teachers can have a direct effect on students' pathways to
the prison pipeline through their relationships with students in the classroom, their
individual responses to student behavior, and their own attitudes, competencies, and
contributions to student learning, (Coggshall, Osher, & Colombi, 2013). All of these factors affect the likelihood that teachers will use harsh and discriminative exclusionary
practices in the classroom. Other studies support the idea that providing additional
training for teachers, especially in areas that are relevant for the student populations
they work with, can effectively begin to disrupt the school-to-prison pipeline from the
ground up (Allen & White-Smith, 2014; Bryan, 2017; Gass & Laughter, 2015).

One way that teachers can begin to disrupt the pipeline is through teaching students about social justice and providing them with the tools and support needed
to enable them to become activists for themselves and their communities (Rubin,
2014). Several studies suggest that youth are explicitly entitled to many basic rights
currently not covered by legislation for educational settings. These may include the
use of the Miranda warning, notice of the right to not self-incriminate, the right

to be represented by an attorney, and other protections currently afforded to juvenile offenders outside of schools (Cobb, 2009; North, 2012; Price, 2009). Bracy (2010) argued that through the use of school resource officers, students' legal rights are diminished, and Price (2009) suggested that school resource officers should be considered police officers to ensure the protection of students' legal rights in schools. School districts and administrators would need to support these changes.

Research shows that it is mostly poor and minority youth who are more likely to face the harsh and discriminatory practices that exclude students, many coming from disadvantaged schools and often living in households with incomes that are below the poverty line, and these students are not likely to have support or access to legal representation to help them when they do face disciplinary procedures. Without adequate representation, many students will not receive fair and just treatment. It is for precisely this reason that Fedders and Langberg (2013) suggested that one step in dismantling the pipeline would be supporting the availability of legal clinics in schools to help both students and their families with a myriad of issues that many of them may face. Some of these issues may include assistance with fair housing and discrimination claims, dealing with employment matters, and addressing family court issues, such as divorce and child support, as well as providing support with governmental benefits, including medical, childcare, and food stamps or Supplemental Nutrition Assistance Program (SNAP) payments.

While teacher education and support for establishing the rights of students can be instrumental in dismantling the school-to-prison pipeline, another important variable to consider is school characteristics and climate. Research shows that schools with high across-the-board suspension rates can be indicative of a highly punitive school climate (Arcia, 2007; Skiba et al., 2014). Studies show that while a punitive school climate can increase the overall rate of exclusionary disciplinary practices, developing connections in schools, building relationships, and establishing bonds between students, teachers, and administrators all work to change the school culture and have a tremendous effect on disrupting the pipeline (Raible & Irizarry, 2010).

Crawford and Burns (2015) found that schools with more than 50% of students who believed that their educational experiences were valuable had significantly lower levels of all forms of violence, indicating that school culture is important to disrupting the pipeline. Castillo (2014) argued that school districts need to establish just and proportionate disciplinary procedures, as well as envision broad school-based changes that are needed to disrupt the pipeline. Restorative justice is one possibility that provides a more holistic approach to interactions between people, and research shows that schools using practices built on the principles of restorative justice have found overwhelmingly positive results (Davis, 2019; Gibson, Wilson, Haight, Kayama, & Marshall, 2014).

Restorative justice has developed over the last several decades, first as a response within the criminal justice system and later in other areas, including schools and educational institutions. Restorative practices focus on harms and needs, use inclusive and collaborative processes, address obligations, and involve all stakeholders in processes focused on restoration (Zehr, 2015). According to Zehr (2015), one of the most significant attributes of restorative justice is the value of respect that guides and directs its policies, programs, procedures, and practices. Establishing high levels of mutual respect in schools between teachers and students can directly influence school culture.

Research finds that alternatives to exclusionary disciplinary practices in schools can reduce racial disproportions in the juvenile justice system, and restorative justice offers an alternative to the harsh and punitive culture currently dominating the juvenile and criminal justice systems (Abudu & Miles, 2018; Davis, 2019; Nicholson-Crotty, Birchmeier, & Valentine, 2009; Wearmouth & Berryman, 2012). Restorative justice offers an opportunity to support a new paradigm for what defines a successful school, one based on inclusiveness, relationships, commitments to building community within schools, and disrupting the school-to-prison pipeline through disciplinary procedures focused on restoration rather than retribution.

A study examining the Oakland Unified School District and the effect of a whole-school approach to restorative justice found that there were significant changes in schools that developed restorative justice policies and practices on-campus. In their report, they noted that student suspensions and expulsions dropped considerably, especially for African American youth whose rates of suspension fell 40% within the first year; the overall discipline gap between white/black students decreased significantly, with 60% of staff and 90% of teachers reporting positive effects from the implementation of restorative justice in their schools; and 76% of student conflicts were successfully mediated (Jain et al., 2014). In addition, based on their data, these researchers found that these changes were also significantly influential in academic outcomes and reported that reading levels in restorative justice schools increased by 128%, chronic absenteeism dropped by 24%, high school dropout rates decreased by 56%, and 4-year graduation rates increased by 60% (Jain et al., 2014). These findings support the potential for restorative justice practices.

SUMMARY

The school-to-prison pipeline is a destructive force that gains steam from a number of different factors. Harsh exclusionary discipline practices disproportionately affect African American students, as well as other minority and marginalized student populations, and become a significant predictor for decreasing student involvement in education. Zero-tolerance policies, including those based on the Gun Free School Act and The Drug Free Act, have all worked to increase the militarization of law enforcement and school resource officers working in our schools in the United States. In addition, an overreliance on policing in schools, racial disparities in school discipline practices, and school characteristics and climate all contribute to the movement of students from schools into the justice system. Teachers are specifically implicated as having a direct influence on student trajectories, and additional training for both teachers and school resource officers, focused on helping them to respond directly to the student populations they serve, can be beneficial in diverting students from the pipeline. In addition, school administrations significantly affect the school-to-prison pipeline through a climate supporting the use of heavy discipline, yet they can also have the greatest impact by providing a paradigm shift in school culture. Restorative justice is one option that offers tremendous possibilities for providing alternatives to exclusionary disciplinary practices in schools. By building inclusive environments that are supportive of relationships and social bonds and using responsive and restorative options, restorative justice can be instrumental in dismantling the school-to-prison pipeline.

DISCUSSION QUESTIONS

1. How do themes of punishment contribute to the school-to-prison pipeline?
2. What is the connection between the school-to-prison pipeline and the prison industrial complex?
3. How has the war on drugs influenced educational settings?
4. What are the strategies for dismantling the school-to-prison pipeline?
5. How do zero-tolerance policies in schools result in exclusionary discipline policies?
6. How do gun-free schools contribute to the school-to-prison pipeline?

REFERENCES

Abudu, N. & Miles, R. (2017). Challenging the status quo: An integrated approach to dismantling the school-to-prison pipeline. *St. Thomas Law Review, 30,* 56–67.

Allen, Q. & White-Smith, K. (2014). "Just as bad as prisons": The challenge of dismantling the school-to-prison pipeline through teacher and community education. *Equity & Excellence in Education, 47*(4), 445–460.

Arcia, E. (2007). Variability in schools' suspension rates of black students. *Journal of Negro Education, 76*(4), 597–608.

Aull, E. H. (2012). Zero tolerance, frivolous juvenile court referrals, and the school-to-prison pipeline: using arbitration as a screening-out method to help plug the pipeline. *Ohio State Journal on Dispute Resolution, 27.*

Bennett, W. J., DiIulio, J. J., Jr., & Walters, J. P. (1996). *Body Count: Moral Poverty—and How to Win America's War against Crime and Drugs.* New York: Simon & Schuster.

Blomberg, T., Bales, W., & Piquero, A. (2012). Is Educational Achievement a Turning Point for Incarcerated Delinquents Across Race and Sex? *Journal of Youth Adolescence, 41,* 202-216.

Bowditch, C. (1993). Getting Rid of Troublemakers: High School Disciplinary Procedures and the Production of dropouts. *Social Problems, 40,* pp. 493-509. http://www.jstor.org/stable/3096864

Bracy, N. (2010). Circumventing the law: Students' rights in schools with police. *Journal of Contemporary Criminal Justice, 26*(3), 294-315.

Bryan, N. (2017). White teachers' role in sustaining the school-to-prison pipeline: Recommendations for teacher education. *Urban Review, 49,* 326-345.

Canadian Council on Learning, (2009). *Lessons in learning: No "drop" in the bucket: The high costs of dropping out.* Retrieved from http://en.copian.ca/library/research/ccl/lessons_learning /no_drop_bucket/no_drop_bucket.pdf

Carter, P., Skiba, R., Arredondo, M. I., & Pollock, M. (2017). You can't fix what you don't look at: Acknowledging race in addressing racial discipline disparities. *Urban Education, 52,* pp. 207-235.

Castillo, J. (2014). Tolerance in schools for Latino students: Dismantling the school-to-prison pipeline. *Harvard Journal of Hispanic Policy, 26,* 43-58.

Cobb, H. (2009). Separate and unequal: The disparate impact of school-based referrals to juvenile court. *Harvard Civil Rights—Civil Liberties Law Review, 44,* 581-596.

Coggshall, J., Osher, D., & Colombi, G. (2013). Enhancing educators' capacity to stop the school-to-prison pipeline. *Family Court Review, 51*(3), 435-444.

Cuellar, A. & Markowitz, S. (2015). School Suspension and the School-to-Prison Pipeline. *International Review of Law and Economics, 43,* 98-106.

Curtis, A. J. (2014). Tracing the school-to-prison pipeline from zero-tolerance policies to juvenile justice dispositions. *Georgetown Law Journal, 102, Geo L.J. 1251.* Retrieved from https://georgetownlawjournal.org/articles/86/tracing-school-to-prison-pipeline-from

Crawford, C., & Burns, R. (2015). Preventing school violence: Assessing armed guardians, school policy, and context. *Policing; Bradford, 38*(4), 631-647.

Davis, F. (2019). *Race and restorative justice: Black lives, healing, and US social transformation.* New York: NY: Skyhorse Publishing, Inc.

Dennis, A. (2017). Decriminalizing childhood. *Fordham Urban Law Review, XLV,* pp. 1-44.

Drug Policy Alliance (n.d.). A brief history on the war on drugs. Retrieved from http://www.drugpolicy.org/issues/brief-history-drug-war

Eitle, T. & Eitle, D. (2018). Inequality, Segregation, and the Overrepresentation of African Americans in School Suspensions. *Sociological Perspectives, 47,* pp. 269-287.

Fedders, B., & Langberg, J. (2013). School-based legal services as a tool in dismantling the school-to-prison pipeline and achieving educational equity. *University of Maryland Law Journal: Race, Religion, Gender, & Class, 13*(2), 212–236.

Gage, N.A., Sugai, G., Lunde, K., & DeLoreto. (2013). Truancy and zero tolerance in high school: Does policy align with practice? *Education and Treatment of Children, 36,* pp. 117–138.

Gass, K., & Laughter, J. (2015). "Can I make any difference?" Gang affiliation, the school-to-prison pipeline, and implications for teachers. *The Journal of Negro Education, 84*(3), 333–347.

Gibson, P., Wilson, R., Haight, W., Kayama, M., & Marshall, J. (2014). The role of race in the out-of-school suspensions of black students: The perspectives of students with suspensions, their parents and educators. *Children and Youth Services Review, 47,* 274–282.

Heitzeg, N. A. (2009). Education or incarceration: Zero tolerance policies and the school to prison pipeline. *Forum on Public Policy.*

Jain, S, Bassey, H., Brown, M. & Preety, K. (2014). Restorative Justice In Oakland Schools Implementation and Impacts: An effective strategy to reduce racially disproportionate discipline, suspensions and improve academic outcomes. *Oakland Unified School District.* Retrieved from https://www.ousd.org/cms/lib07/CA01001176/Centricity/Domain/134/OUSDRJ%20Report%20revised%20Final.pdf

Krezmien M. P., Leone, P. E., Zablocki, M. S., & Wells, C. S. (2010). Juvenile court referrals and the public schools: Nature and extent of the practice in five states. *Journal of Contemporary Criminal Justice, 26,* 273.

Lynch, C., Gainey, R., & Chappell, A. (2016). The effects of social and educational disadvantage on the roles and functions of school resource officers. *Policing; Bradford, 39*(3), 521–535.

Mallett, C. (2016). The school-to-prison pipeline: A critical review of the punitive paradigm shift. *Child Adolescence, 33,* pp. 15–24. Retrieved from https://doi.org/10.1007/s10560-015-0397-1

Martinez-Prather, K., McKenna, J., & Bowman, S., (2016). The Impact of Training on Discipline Outcomes in School-Based Policing. *Policing; Bradford, 39,*(3), 478–490.

McCarter, S. (2016). The school-to-prison pipeline: A primer for social workers. *Social Work, 62*(1), 53–61. doi: 10.1093/sw/sww078

McGrew, K. (2016). The dangers of pipeline thinking: How the school-to-prison pipeline metaphor squeezes out complexity. *Educational Theory, 66*(3), 341–367.

McNeal, L. (2016). Managing our blind spot: The role of bias in the school-to-prison pipeline. *Arizona State Law Journal, 48,* 285–311.

Mizel, M., Miles, J., Pedersen, E., Tucker, J., Ewing, B., & D'Amico, E. (2016). To educate or to incarcerate: Factors in disproportionality on school discipline. *Children and Youth Services Review, 70,* 102–111. https://doi.org/10.1016/j.childyouth.2016.09.009

Mongan, P. & Walker, R. (2012). "The road to hell is paved with good intentions": A historical, theoretical, and legal analysis of zero-tolerance weapons policies in American Schools. *Preventing School Failure, 56,* pp. 232–240. https://doi.org/10.1080/1045988X.2011.654366

Monterastelli, S. (2017). Every hand's a loser: The intersection of zero-tolerance policies, mental illness in children and a dolescents, and the juvenile justice system. *Law & Psychology Review, 41,* 209–228.

Moriearty, P. L. & Carson, W. (2012). Cognitive warfare and young Black males in America. *Journal of Gender, Race & Justice, 15,* 281–315.

Moyer, M. (2017). Schoolyard felons: Missouri's new criminal code and its impact on schools. *Missouri Law Review, 82,* pp. 1213–1233.

Na, C. (2017). The consequence of school dropout among serious adolescent offenders: More offending? More arrest? Both? *Journal of Research in Crime and Delinquency, 54,* 78–110.

National Association for the Advancement of Colored People. (n.d.). Criminal justice fact sheet. Retrieved from http://www.naacp.org/criminal-justice-fact-sheet/

National Center for Education Statistics. (2015). Public school safety and discipline: 2013–14, First look. *Institute of Education Sciences.* Retrieved from https://nces.ed.gov/pubs2015/2015051.pdf

Nicholson-Crotty, S., Birchmeier, Z., & Valentine, D. (2009). Exploring the impact of school discipline on racial disproportion in the juvenile justice system. *Social Science Quarterly, 90*(4), 1003–1018.

North, K. (2012). Recess is over: Granting Miranda rights to students interrogated inside school walls. *Emory Law Journal, 62,* 441–482.

Novak, A. (2018). The association between experiences of exclusionary discipline and justice system contact: A systematic review. *Aggression and Violent Behavior, 40,* 73–82. Doi.org/10.1016/j.avb.2018.04.002

Peak, B. (2015). Militarization of School Police: One Route on the School-to-Prison Pipeline. *Arkansas Law Review, 68,* 195–229.

Perry, B. & Morris, E. (2014). Suspending Progress: Collateral Consequences of Exclusionary Punishment in Public Schools. *American Sociological review, 76*(6), 1067–1087.

Price, P. (2009). When is a police officer an officer of the law: The status of police officers in schools. *The Journal of Criminal Law and Criminology, 99*(2), 541–570.

Public Broadcasting Station. (n.d.). Thirty years of America's drug war: A chronology. Retrieved from https://www.pbs.org/wgbh/pages/frontline/shows/drugs/cron/

Raible, J., & Irizarry, J. (2010). Redirecting the teacher's gaze: Teacher education, youth surveillance, and the school-to-prison pipeline. *Teaching and Teacher Education, 26,* 1196–1203. doi:10.1016/j.tate.2010.02.006

Rich, L. (2016). "CERD-AIN" reform: Dismantling the school-to-prison pipeline through more thorough coordination of the departments of justice and education. *Loyola of Los Angeles Law Review, 49,* 119–189.

Rocque, M. (2010). Office discipline and student behavior: Does race matter? *American Journal of Education, 116,* pp. 557–581.

Rubin, D. (2014). Engaging Latino/a students in the secondary English classroom: A step toward breaking the school-to-prison pipeline. *Journal of Latinos and Education, 13*, 222–230.

Ruiz, R. R. (2017) School-to-prison pipeline: An evaluation of zero tolerance policies and their alternatives. *Houston Law Review, 54*(3), 803–837.

Skiba, R. (2013). Reaching a Critical Juncture for Our Kids: The Need to Reassess School Justice Practices. *Family Court Review, 51*(3), 380–387.

Skiba, R., Choong-Geun, C., Trachok, M., Baker, T., Sheya, A., & Hughes, R. (2014). Parsing disciplinary disproportionality: Contributions of infraction, student, and school characteristics to out-of-school suspension and expulsion. *American Educational Research Journal, 51*(4), 640–670.

Snapp, S., Hoenig, J., Fields, A., & Russell, S. (2015). Messy, butch, and queer: LGBTQ youth and the school-to-prison pipeline. *Journal of Adolescent Research, 30*(1), 57–82.

Theriot, M. (2009). School Resource Officers and the Criminalization of Student Behavior. *Journal of Criminal Justice, 37*(3), 280–287.

Wallace, J., Goodkind, S., Wallace, C. & Bachman, J. (2008). Racial, Ethnic, and Gender Differences in School Discipline among U.S. High School Students: 1991-2005. *Negro Educational Review, 59*(1–2): 47–62.

Wearmouth, J. & Berrymman, M. (2012). Viewing restorative approaches to addressing challenging behavior of minority ethnic students through a community of practice lens. *Cambridge Journal of Education, 42*(2), 253–268.

Welch, K. & Payne, A. (2010). Racial threat and punitive school discipline. *Social Problems, 57*, pp. 25–48.

White, B. (2018). The Invisible Victims of the School-to-Prison Pipeline: Understanding Black Girls, School Push-Out, and the Impact of the "Every Student Succeeds" Act. *William & Mary Journal of Women and the Law, 24*, 641–663

Wilson, H. (2014). Turning off the school-to-prison pipeline. *Reclaiming Children and Youth, 23*(1), 49–53.

Zehr, H. (2015). *The little book of restorative justice.* New York: NY: Skyhorse Publishing, Inc.

CHAPTER FOUR

Racial and Gender Disparities in Schools and Juvenile Justice Involvement

Doshie Piper, J. Renee Trombley, and Danielle Alsandor

READING OBJECTIVES

- Expose the reader to the racial and gender disproportionality in school discipline practices.
- Highlight the existing research on school disciplinary practices and inequality.
- Examine research on racial and gender patterns in school sanctions and consider how disproportionate discipline might contribute to low academic achievement among students of color.
- Critically consider the implications that racial and gender inequalities in school discipline have on juvenile justice involvement.

OVERVIEW

There continues to be an overrepresentation of boys in school disciplinary sanctions. Historical and contemporary research on school disciplinary practices shows that boys are referred to the office and receive a range of disciplinary consequences at higher rates than girls (Lietz and Gregory, 1978; McFadden, Marsh, Price, and Hwang, 1992; Shaw & Braden, 1990; Skiba, Peterson, & Williams, 1997; Skiba, Michael, Nardo, & Peterson, 2002; Taylor & Foster, 1986). For example, an examination of U.S. Office for Civil Rights data from 1992 found that boys are more than 4 times as likely as girls to be referred to the office, suspended, or subjected to corporal punishment (Gregory, 1996). More specifically, this data revealed a gender-by-race

THE RACIAL AND GENDER DISPARITY IN SCHOOLS

By Shanda Glover

Please click on this hyperlink to access the article:

https://uiwomenscenter.wordpress.com/2016/03/28/the-racial-and-gender-disparity-in-schools/

Or scan the QR code with your cell phone to view the article:

intersection in the probability of receiving school discipline. Gregory (1996) found that black males were 16 times more likely to receive corporal punishment than white females. Moreover, Taylor and Foster (1986) examined disciplinary responses at both the middle and high school levels and reported a consistent ordering in the likelihood of suspension by racial and gender demographics from most to least with black males receiving the most suspensions, followed by white males, then black females, and, lastly, white females.

Research shows that it was not until 1994 that national data was disaggregated by gender and race to determine differences in rates and to assess disparities. In 1995, one of the first articles to examine racial and gender differences in corporal punishment published significant findings supporting the fact that African American males were most likely to be disciplined through the use of corporal punishment taking place in U.S. public schools (Gregory, 1995). The overwhelming evidence that Black boys are treated differently when it comes to school discipline leads many to question the trajectory that leads to these practices (Gibson, Wilson, Haight, Kayama, & Marshall, 2014).

These racial and gendered statistics on school discipline should not come at a surprise within the current school climate. The presence of police officers in schools often informs how educational systems have shifted from a discretionary student disciplinary framework to a crime control orientation (Kupchik 2010; Hirschfield & Celinska, 2011). In other words, if schools rely heavily on policing practices opposed to or instead of mutually working together to identify what works for specific students. Take, for example, the article in the sidebar published by the University of Idaho Women's Center's blog written by Shanda Glover, a high school student who highlights the current school disciplinary practices for females of color.

SCHOOL DISCIPLINE PRACTICES AND POLICIES

According to the U.S. Department of Education (2014), black students consisted of 16% of school enrollment; this small percentage made up 72% of students referred to law enforcement and 31% of students who experience a school-related arrest. Some research showed that being black disadvantages girls more than it does boys in school discipline practices (Crenshaw, Ocen, & Nanda 2015). Black females are suspended 6 times more often than white females, and black females represent the fastest growing population within the juvenile justice system (Crenshaw et al., 2015). These school disciplinary practices extend beyond the black female students directly involved in the disciplinary infraction. Figure 4.1 demonstrates the disproportional racial and ethnic disparities that exist in school discipline.

It also has a negative effect on their peers who witness the unfair disciplinary practices. As a result, these students rebel or disengage when they witness institutional practices and societal hypocrisy that contradicts the principles of civility, respect, and fairness that educational institutions promote (Preiss, Arum, Edelman, Morrill, & Tyson, 2015). Ruth-Manuel Logan notes an example of these disciplinary practices in the article in the sidebar.

School Practices or Policies on Minority and Other Marginalized Groups

Research shows that black girls have faced stigma in society and in schools that often characterizes their behavior as unruly, defiant, having bad attitudes, and being unsophisticated, yet the research often ignores the specific implication for black girls pushed into the school-to-prison pipeline (White, 2018). Additional research notes that teachers often label certain youth as "troublemakers," when in reality, these students are often facing significant challenges at home and in their communities. Yet these labels reinforce negative stigma around the youth and can divert and transform thoughts

THIS GRANDMA THINKS THE SCHOOL DISTRICT WENT TOO FAR

By Ruth-Manuel Logan on August 6, 2014

Please click on this hyperlink to access the article:

https://magicbaltimore.com/3407340/this-grandma-thinks-the-school-district-went-too-far/

Or scan the QR code with your cell phone to view the article:

PERCENTAGE OF PUBLIC SCHOOL STUDENTS WHO RECEIVED OUT-OF-SCHOOL SUSPENSIONS, BY RACE/ETHNICITY AND SEX: 2013–14

RACE/ETHNICITY	MALE	FEMALE	TOTAL
Black/African American	17.6%	9.6%	13.7%
American Indian/Alaska Native	9.1%	4.3%	6.7%
Two or more races	7.4%	3.1%	5.3%
Hispanic/Latino of any race	6.4%	2.6%	4.5%
Native Hawaiian/Other Pacific Islander	6.2%	2.7%	4.5%
White	5.0%	1.7%	3.4%
Asian	1.7%	0.5%	1.1%
Total	7.3%	3.2%	5.3%

FIGURE 4.1 Adapted from: Indicator 15: Retention, Suspension and Expulsion, Status and Trends in the Education of Racial and Ethnic Groups, National Center for Education Statistics (2019)

about a student needing services to thoughts of a student deserving punishment (Bowditch, 2018).

School resources, the quality of teaching and curriculum, quality of relationship with parents, and community all contribute to school performance. Low-performing and high-poverty schools produce higher dropout rates. High-poverty schools are often producing students who are expected to remain poor. Across the United States, 1,700 schools are responsible for almost half of all students who leave high school without a diploma, and 75% of these students are minority (Tucci, 2009). Nearly 58% of the students who left one of the nation's high-poverty, low-performing schools were Black and Latino (Tucci, 2009). Black girls under the age of 18 make up 35% of the poverty rate, and Black girls drop out of school 7% more than white girls, who drop out at 3.8% (US Census Bureau, 2010). This suggests that a higher percentage of Black students who dropped out were likely struggling in school.

Students who deal with learning and behavioral disabilities are more likely to be labeled as problem students, more likely to be referred to the office, and more likely to receive the severest penalties possible for very minor infractions. The use of high-stakes testing has been implicated in the school-to-prison pipeline, as research suggests that low-performing youth may often be "pushed out," and in one study, 25% of students who had been labeled as dropping out actually reported being "discharged coercively" (Bowditch, 2018). The No Child Left Behind Act, enacted by Congress in 2001, provided legislation meant to ensure that schools were held accountable for student performance but had the unintended effect of changing the landscape of educational practices with tragic consequences for student learning. This legislation prioritized high-stakes testing and an educational climate that linked assessment of students' learning to a single measure of test performance. Students of color were disproportionately affected by grade retention as a result of this practice (Au, 2016).

National standardized tests reveal racial disparities among girls (Curry, 2014). Controversial, single measures of knowledge may deter Black girls from continuing their education or lead them to internalize that school is not for them.

Scully (2016) argued that this policy of using scores on standardized testing as a metric for school success has led schools to hyper focus on testing with the result that "no longer is learning a lifetime endeavor and a key to quality education … instead, learning is encouraged primarily for the purpose of passing a test." (Scully, 2016, p. 1001) In addition to decreasing educational opportunities that have a significant effect on life-course variables, students who have academic difficulties and poor performance on exams are more likely to be targeted for disciplinary actions, including transfers to alternative schools, further increasing their risk of engaging with the juvenile justice system (Scully, 2016). Additional research on standardized testing suggests that many of these instruments are inherently biased against racial and ethnic minorities (Smith, 2009). While the importance of labels and stigma on the school-to-prison pipeline cannot be ignored, more research is needed to explore fully the effect this has on diverse groups of students and in different educational settings.

However, there is considerable research examining the disproportionate number of African American boys being funneled through the school-to-prison pipeline. In fact, research overwhelmingly finds that African American boys suffer the most from exclusionary disciplinary practices in schools (Rich, 2016). In 2009, research supported by the National Institute of Health argued that disparities in the treatment of African American youth in school disciplinary procedures have been evident in research since the 1970s. Their research found evidence of disproportionate rates of exclusionary school discipline practices, including suspensions and expulsions, which have continued over the last several decades (Wallace, Goodkind, Wallace, & Bachman, 2008).

Teachers are overwhelmingly implicated in these disparities based on the unequal treatment of students in the classroom and differences in referrals to the office for disciplinary action. One study found that even when the offenses that were committed were exactly the same, black students were significantly more likely to receive harsh punitive exclusionary discipline compared to white students, and in that study, the authors noted that it is exactly these types of disciplinary practices that were more likely to increase the risk of black youth landing up in the juvenile justice system (Nicholson-Crotty, Birchmeier, & Valentine, 2009). The connections between the classroom to the courtroom have become tragic for many of today's youth, and teachers have played a key role.

Research shows that overarching teacher surveillance of black youth in the classroom combined with a lack of training for teachers who work with diverse and underserved minority populations, especially in urban areas, increases teachers' implicit bias in exclusionary disciplinary practices (Raible & Irizarry, 2010). The reality is that many teachers lack an understanding of how their actions affect the school-to-prison pipeline, how their actions have a direct effect on the criminalization of youth in schools, and how in their roles as teachers they are overwhelmingly responsible for contributing, in large part, to the growth and development of the school-to-prison pipeline, including the resulting disparities seen within the juvenile justice system.

Minority Female Experiences with Punitive Policies in Educational Environments

The number of girls who experienced one or more out-of-school suspension decreased between 2000 and 2009 from 871,176 to 849,447 (Oswald, Best, Coutinho, & Nagle, 2003). The racial disparities remain. Black girls are nearly 16% of girls enrolled in schools, yet their rate of discipline has remained elevated. Black girls were 34% of girls who experienced out-of-school suspension. Black girls represented 43% of girls suspended during the 2006 school year. By the 2009 school year, Black girls represented 52% of all girls with multiple out-of-school suspensions (Rycroft-Smith & Andre, 2019). The 2011–2012 school year had 18 states with out-of-school suspensions rates higher than 12% the national average (U.S. Department of Education, 2014). The use of exclusionary discipline was 24% for southern Black girls; however, 75% of these girls received out-of- school suspension.

The 2009–2010 school year produced 31% Black girls referred to law enforcement and 43% school-based arrest (Oswald et al., 2003). In 2011–2012 the percentage stayed the same, while school-based arrests decreased to 34%. The rate at which Black girls experience harsh school discipline is disproportionate (Oswald et al., 2003). Nationwide, Black girls were 38% of all girls arrested, which is nearly four times higher than white females. Nationally, Black female students were referred to law enforcement at a rate of 43%, two and half times more than white female students. Black girls in charter schools make up 29% of the enrollment, but 35% of referrals to law enforcement, 52% of girls placed in restraints, and 45% of girls arrested on-campus (Kelly, 2018).

Black girls are those who curse, drink, fight, steal, and lie. These labels have built the "bad" Black girls who participate in underground economies and have been sent to group homes, training schools, and detention facilities to transform them into "good girls." The African American Policy Forum and UCLA School of Law agree that black girls and other girls of color face harsh punitive policies in educational environments, so much so that they supported focus groups in Boston and New York City conducted by the Center for Intersectionality and Social Policy Studies between September 2012 and August 2013. The observations are as follows:

1. In New York and Boston, black boys and girls were subject to larger achievement gaps and harsher forms of discipline than their white counterparts. On some measures, the relative magnitude of the racial disparity between girls is greater than the disparity between boys.

2. At-risk young women describe zero-tolerance schools as chaotic environments in which discipline is prioritized over educational attainment. Participants indicated that zero-tolerance environments are neither safe nor conducive to learning. On the contrary, the emphasis on discipline leads many girls to become disengaged from the learning process and from school altogether.

3. Increased levels of law enforcement and security personnel within schools sometimes make girls feel less safe and less likely to attend school. Some of the young women reported that their discomfort with security rituals, such as passing through metal detectors, was so great that they were dissuaded from coming to school at all.

4. Girls' attachment and sense of belonging in school can be undermined if their achievements are overlooked or undervalued. Research suggests that black girls sometimes get less attention than their male counterparts early in their school careers because they are perceived to be more socially mature and self-reliant. The lack of attention can lead to "benign neglect" that may diminish school attachment in both high- and moderate-achieving female students.

5. Punitive rather than restorative responses to conflict contribute to the separation of girls from school and to their disproportionate involvement in the juvenile justice system. Several participants indicated that they were suspended or *expelled* and some even *prosecuted* for fighting in school. Conflicts that might have been better addressed through counseling or other conflict resolution strategies were instead referred to the juvenile justice system.

6. The failure of schools to intervene in situations involving the sexual harassment and bullying of girls contributes to their insecurity at school. Stakeholders and participants noted that a heavy emphasis on discipline does little to curb harassing behavior in schools. Instead, zero-tolerance policies may exacerbate the vulnerability of girls to harassing behavior because it penalizes them for defending themselves against such acts.

7. Girls sometimes resort to "acting out" when their counseling needs are overlooked or disregarded. In environments in which discipline is emphasized over counseling, girls who struggle with trauma and other unmet needs may come to the attention of school personnel only when their behavior leads to punishable offenses.

8. School-age black girls experience a high incidence of interpersonal violence. Among the factors that disrupted some of the participants' ability to finish school were trauma associated with sexual assault and other forms of violence.

9. Black and Latina girls are often burdened with familial obligations that undermine their capacity to achieve their academic goals. Many stakeholders noted that girls were much more likely to be faced with caretaking responsibilities

that compromised their ability to pursue their academic goals than their male counterparts.

10. Pregnancy and parenting make it difficult for girls to engage fully in school. Pregnant girls are burdened by early parenthood in ways that boys are not. They are segregated from their peers and stigmatized in a manner that may undermine their attachment to school.

JUVENILE JUSTICE IMPLICATIONS OF SCHOOL DISCIPLINARY PRACTICES

In addition to the influence teachers have from the classroom, there is significant evidence that factors such as the rate of low-income students in schools and the large number of students from minority populations indicate an increase in risk for the regular use of harsh disciplinary procedures in schools, most often affecting young black males (Nance, 2013). Research also shows that schools and districts with higher rates of black students in their population were more likely to use harsher disciplinary practices compared with schools and districts with lower minority populations, which were more likely to rely on medicalized treatment and practices for their disruptive student populations (Ramey, 2015).

Nance (2013) furthered the conversation by providing support for the idea that these intense security measures and harsh and exclusionary disciplinary strategies only cause more harm through the creation of barriers between students and teachers and by exacerbating underlying problems without really resolving the serious issues. In addition, during a systematic review of the research on harsh exclusionary penalties and disciplinary practices, researchers found that these practices directly funnel youth into the juvenile justice system and provided support showing that significant associations were present between these types of school-based penalties and further interactions with the juvenile justice system (Novak, 2018). In examining school-based referrals to the juvenile justice system, one report noted that in some cases, up to 10% of referrals were being made at the school level and that schools continue to be contributors to the overrepresentation of African American youth in the juvenile justice system.

In fact, research found that school referrals to the juvenile justice system have increased considerably over the last two decades, thus having direct implications on the overincarceration of youth in the United States. One of the ways this has taken place is directly through the proliferation of law enforcement and school resource officers within the school system, implemented to provide security and law enforcement during both regular school hours and after-school events, yet many argue that this has actually led to the overcriminalization of youth and the growth of the school-to-prison pipeline (Price, 2009; Theriot, 2009).

RACIAL DISPARITIES IN JUVENILE JUSTICE

In 2019, there were almost 50,000 youth incarcerated in the juvenile justice system including those housed in detention centers (16,858), residential treatment centers (10,256), long-term secure facilities (10,777), group homes (3,375), and adult prisons and jails (4,535), with the remaining youth being housed in reception and diagnostic facilities, shelters, boot camps, and ranch and wilderness camps (Sawyer, 2019). Research examining the disparities in detainment and incarceration rates of juveniles continues to find evidence of disproportionate minority contact. When examining the most recent data, Black youth continue to be significantly overrepresented in the number of youth currently confined in correctional facilities in the United States. Reports show that even though Black youth make up only 14% of the juvenile population under 18 years of age, Black boys represent 42%, and Black girls account for 35% of the total juvenile population detained in correctional facilities (Sawyer, 2019). Studies show that variations in racial disparities are often found when looking at different states and regions, with other marginalized populations also facing disproportionate contact with the juvenile justice system, including those who identify as Hispanic youth as well as Native American youth.

The data surrounding this disproportionate minority contact for youth is overwhelmingly disturbing. While reports show that the overall incarceration rates in juvenile justice fell 54% between 2001 and 2015, the decline in incarceration has not been equally distributed. During this time, the racial disparity between white and Black youth increased by 22%, and while the national rate of incarceration among youth was 152 per 100,000, the rate for white youth was much lower, at 86 per 100,000, and the rate for Black youth significantly higher at 433 per 100,000 (Rovner, 2014). Looking at disparities in offenses shows simple but significant differences. For instance, when compared with white youth, Black youth are 269 times more likely to be arrested for curfew violations (Rovner). These disparities are seen at every level of the juvenile justice system and continue for these youth, many times following them into the adult criminal justice system.

Studies surrounding race and gender differences in juvenile justice have shown substantial differences at every point of contact, including policing, courts, and corrections. An overview of these studies suggests the need for more research engaging in an intersectional framework in order to capture the differences among racial and gender identities and shows how this impacts individual experiences in the juvenile justice system (Peck, Leiber, Beaudry-Cyr, & Toman, 2015). It is imperative to examine the different pathways that youth travel on their way to the juvenile justice system. Discussions on pathways for marginalized groups are important for the field, especially in consideration of youth with multiple marginalized identities, and how these identities pose different risk and protective factors across the life course. Understanding the impact of racial identity on juvenile justice involvement can help inform evidence-based policies and practices for reducing the high rates of disparity we see in the system.

GENDER DISPARITIES IN JUVENILE JUSTICE

While the rate of detention has decreased for boys, the rates have increased for girls (Casey Foundation, 2013). Between 1996 and 2011, the proportion of girls arrested declined by 42% compared to 57% decline for boys (Sherman & Balck, 2015). Thirty-seven percent of girls were detained for status offenses and technical violations, while 25% of boys were for status offenses and technical violations, rather than for delinquent acts that posed a danger to school or public safety (Sherman & Balck, 2015). Girls are 21% more likely than boys (12%) to be detained for sexual assault and public disorder cases, including those that include public drunkenness or school scuffles (Sherman & Balck, 2015). These data represent the number of girls who do not present an immediate threat to the public or educational environment but are confined in juvenile correctional facilities, despite the negative impact of detention on educational achievement (Holman & Ziedenberg, 2006).

More than 70% of girls in juvenile detention facilities have a history of trauma, and at least 60% have experienced rape or the threat of rape. These numbers represent the reported incidents and do not account for the instances of sexual assault that are unaccounted for. These number do not account for the number of girls in detention who had gang involvement. Empirical research has characterized female gang involvement like that of male gang involvement (Campbell, 1984; Moore, 1988). These studies suggest that females involved with gangs have a history of emotional, physical, and sexual abuse, come from dysfunctional homes and families, and fall below the poverty line. Female gang involvement could induce a range of life factors that will have a future impact, such as performing poorly in school, dropping out of school, possibly getting pregnant, becoming a teenage mother, engaging in drug and alcohol use, and juvenile confinement (Sanchez & Rodriguez, 2008).

In the late 1990s the Blossom Program for girls was launched in New York at the Youth Empowerment Mission. Girls who were gang-involved or had other contact with the juvenile justice system received support. The Blossom Program, which is now in schools in New York, once facilitated the recovery process for more than 2,000 girls and their families that were confined in New York's juvenile department of corrections (Morris, 2016). Most of the girls in the program were looking for a rehabilitation from their substance dependencies and addiction to violence. After being involved in the program, it was discovered that these girls were actually responding to much more trauma.

Correctional information about Black girls have been based on their positions to Black males and White females. The juvenile justice system has never developed clear pathways to success for Black girls in confinement. This has now come back to threaten the legitimacy of the juvenile justice system that is supposed to prevent future involvement with criminal justice system (Morris, 2016). This racial and gender disparity in juvenile justice is the function of many factors: unemployment and poverty, poor school performance and truancy, and, most importantly, differential handling, lack of gender responsive treatment, and alternatives to detention (Morris, 2016). Between 1997 and 2011, Black girls experienced assignment to residential placement at a rate of 123 per 100,000, one of the highest in the nation (Sickmund, 2000). This racial isolation, coupled with an increase in the number of girls being placed in these facilities, impacts the development of an effective culturally competent learning continuum for Black girls.

Many teachers in juvenile correctional facilities care about the education of the students in the detention facility. However, many teachers express feeling overwhelmed and often emotionally unprepared. They have also admitted to feeling insufficiently trained to deal with the countless issues that prevent them from forming meaningful relationships, even if only temporary, with the girls they educate in juvenile detention (Morris, 2016). Juvenile court schools do not serve to repair the harm already done by traditional schools. Students find the work to be repetitive and unrelated to their interests and goals. Most instructors are punitive and impatient. A study completed by the U.S. Department of Education found that 43% of incarcerated youth received remedial education services in detention and did not return to school after their release (LeBlanc & Ratnofsky, 1991). Sixteen percent of the confined youth returned to school after their release but dropped out five months later (LeBlanc & Ratnofsky, 1991). Histories of victimization and addiction, poor student–teacher relationships, being subject to zero-tolerance and harsh discipline with poorly executed curriculum, and the schools' mismatched system functioned to push Black girls in juvenile court schools and further away from all schooling.

DISCUSSION QUESTIONS

1. What is the racial and gender disproportionality in school discipline practices?
2. What does the existing research on school disciplinary practices say about inequality?
3. How does the research on racial and gender patterns in school sanctions consider how disproportionate discipline might contribute to low academic achievement among students of color?
4. What are the implications that racial and gender inequality in school discipline have on juvenile justice involvement?

REFERENCES

Annie E. Casey Foundation. (2013). *Reducing youth incarceration in the United States.* Baltimore, MD: Author.

Au, W. (2016). Meritocracy 2.0: High-stakes, standardized testing as a racial project of neo-liberal multiculturalism. *Educational Policy, 30*(1), 39–62.

Bowditch, C. (2018). Getting rid of troublemakers: High school disciplinary procedures and the production of dropouts. *Social Problems, 40*(4), 493–509. Retrieved from http://www.jstor.org/stable/3096864

Campbell, A. (1984). Girls' talk: The social representation of aggression by female gang members. *Criminal justice and behavior,* 11(2), 139–156.

Crenshaw, K., Ocen, P., & Nanda, J. (2015). *Black girls matter: Pushed out, overpoliced and underprotected.* New York, NY: African American Policy Forum, Center for Intersectionality and Social Policy Studies.

Curry, D. L. (2014). *The impact of teacher quality on reading achievement of fourth grade students: An analysis of the 2007, 2009, 2011, and 2013 National Assessment of Educational Progress (NAEP).* University of North Texas.

Gibson, P., Wilson, R., Haight, W., Kayama, M., & Marshall, J. (2014). The role of race in the out-of-school suspensions of black students: The perspectives of students with suspensions, their parents and educators. *Children and youth services review, 47,* 274–282.

Gregory, J. F. (1996). The crime of punishment: Racial and gender disparities in the use of corporal punishment in the U.S. public schools. *Journal of Negro Education, 64,* 454–462.

Hirschfield, P. J., & Celinska, K. (2011). Beyond fear: Sociological perspectives on the criminalization of school discipline. *Sociology Compass, 5*(1), 1–12. doi:10.1111/j.1751-9020.2010.00342.x

Holman, B., & Ziedenberg, J. (2006). *The dangers of detention.* Washington, DC: Justice Policy Institute.

Kelly, L. L. (2018). A snapchat story: How black girls develop strategies for critical resistance in school. *Learning, Media and Technology, 43*(4), 374–389.

Kupchik, A. (2010). *Homeroom security: School discipline in an age of fear.* New York, NY: New York University Press.

LeBlanc, L.A & Ratnofsky, A. (1991). *Unlocking learning: Chapter 1 in correctional facilities.* Washington, DC: U.S. Department of Education. Office of the Under Secretary.

Lietz, J. J., & Gregory, M. K. (1978). Pupil race and sex determinants of office and exceptional education referrals. *Educational Research Quarterly, 3*(2), 61–66.

McFadden, A. C., Marsh, G. E., Price, B. J., & Hwang, Y. (1992). A study of race and gender bias in the punishment of handicapped school children. *Urban Review, 24,* 239–251.

Moore, J. W. (1988). *Changing Chicano gangs: Acculturation, generational change, evolution of deviance or emerging underclass?* Los Angeles, CA: University of California Los Angeles, Institute for Social Science Research.

Morris, M. (2016). *Pushout: The criminalization of Black girls in schools.* New York, NY: The New Press.

Nance, J. (2013). Students, security, and race. *Emory Law Journal, 63*, 1–57.

Nicholson-Crotty, S., Birchmeier, Z., & Valentine, D. (2009). Exploring the impact of school discipline on racial disproportion in the juvenile justice system. *Social Science Quarterly, 90*(4), 1003–1018.

Novak, A. (2018). The association between experiences of exclusionary discipline and justice system contact: A systematic review. *Aggression and Violent Behavior, 40*, 73–82. doi,org/10.1016/j.avb.2018.04.002

Oswald, D. P., Best, A. M., Coutinho, M. J., & Nagle, H. A. (2003). Trends in the special education identification rates of boys and girls: A call for research and change. *Exceptionality, 11*(4), 223–237.

Peck, J. H., Leiber, M. J., Beaudry-Cyr, M. & Toman, E. L. (2015). The conditioning effects of race and gender on the juvenile court outcomes of delinquent and "neglected" types of offenders. *Justice Quarterly, 33*, 1210–1236.

Preiss, D. R., Arum, R., Edelman, L. B., Morrill C., & Tyson, K. (2015). The more you talk, the worse it is: Student perceptions of law and authority in schools. *Social Currents, 3*(3), 234–255.

Price, P. (2009). When is a police officer an officer of the law: The status of police officers in schools. *The Journal of Criminal Law and Criminology, 99*(2), 541–570.

Raible, J., & Irizarry, J. (2010). Redirecting the teacher's gaze: Teacher education, youth surveillance, and the school-to-prison pipeline. *Teaching and Teacher Education, 26*, 1196–1203. doi:10.1016/j.tate.2010.02.006

Ramey, D. (2015). The social structure of criminalized and medicalized school discipline. *American Sociological Association, 88*(3), 181–201.doi:10:1177/00380407/15587114

Rich, L. (2016). "CERD-AIN" reform: Dismantling the school-to-prison pipeline through more thorough coordination of the departments of justice and education. *Loyola of Los Angeles Law Review, 49*, 119–189.

Rovner, J. (2014). Policy Brief: Disproportionate Minority Contact. Retrieved from https://www.sentencingproject.org/publications/disproportionate-minority-contact-in-the-juvenile-justice-system/

Rycroft-Smith, L., & Andre, G. (Eds.). (2019). The equal classroom: Life-changing thinking about gender. Routledge.

Sanchez, R., & Rodriguez, S. (2008). *Lady Q: the rise and fall of a Latin queen.* Chicago, IL: Chicago Review Press.

Sawyer, W. (2019). Youth confinement: The whole pie 2019. Retrieved from Prison Policy Initiative website http://www.prisonpolicy.org/reports/youth2019.html

Scully, J. (2016). Examining and dismantling the school-to-prison pipeline: Strategies for a better future. *Arkansas Law Review, 68*, 959–1010.

Shaw, S. R., & Braden, J. P. (1990). Race and gender bias in the administration of corporal punishment. *School Psychology Review, 19*, 378–383.

Sherman, F., & Balck, A. (2015). *Gender injustice: System-level juvenile justice reforms for girls.* Portland, OR: The National Crittenton Foundation.

Sickmund, M. (2000). *Census of juveniles in residential placement databook.* US Department of Justice, Office of Justice Programs, Office of Juvenile Justice and Delinquency Prevention.

Skiba, R. J., Michael, R. S., Nardo, A. C., & Peterson, R. L. (2002). The color of discipline: Sources of racial and gender disproportionality in school punishment. *Urban Review, 34,* 317–342.

Skiba, R. J., Peterson, R. L., & Williams, T. (1997). Office referrals and suspension: Disciplinary intervention in middle schools. *Education and Treatment of Children, 20*(3), 295–315.

Smith, C. (2009). Deconstructing the pipeline: Evaluating protection cases through a structural racism framework. *Fordham Urban Law Journal, 36,* 1009–1049.

Taylor, M. C., & Foster, G. A. (1986). Bad boys and school suspensions: Public policy implications for black males. *Sociological Inquiry, 56,* 498–506.

Theriot, M. (2009). School resource officers and the criminalization of student behavior. *Journal of Criminal Justice, 37*(3), 280–287.

Tucci, T. (2009). *Prioritizing the nation's dropout factories.* Washington, DC: Alliance for Excellent Education.

U.S. Census Bureau. (2010). *People in Families by Family Structure, Age, and Sex, Iterated by Income-to-Poverty Ratio and Race: 2009.* Washington, DC.

U.S. Department of Education. (2014). *Guiding principles: A resource guide for improving school climate and discipline.* Washington, DC. Retrieved from https://www2.ed.gov/policy/gen/guid/school-discipline/guiding-principles.pdf

U.S. Department of Education Office for Civil Rights. (2014). *Civil rights data collection data snapshot: School discipline* (Issue brief no. 1). Washington, DC.

Wallace, J., Goodkind, S., Wallace, C., & Bachman, J. (2008). Racial, ethnic, and gender differences in school discipline among U.S. high school students: 1991–2005. *Negro Educational Review, 59*(1–2), 47–62.

White, B. (2018). The invisible victims of the school-to-prison pipeline: Understanding black girls, school push-out, and the impact of the "Every Student Succeeds" Act. *William & Mary Journal of Women and the Law, 24,* 641–663

Figure Credit

Fig. 4.1: Source: U.S. Department of Education, Office for Civil Rights, Civil Rights Data Collection, 2011-2012.

CHAPTER FIVE

Policing Schools

Doshie Piper and J. Renee Trombley

READING OBJECTIVES

- Understand how police presence in schools started.
- Discuss the significance of the Safe School Act of 1994.
- Understand how the Gun-Free Schools Act of 1994 affected education agencies.
- Examine strategies for implementing school resource officers.

OVERVIEW

This chapter examines police presence in schools. The effects and implications that police presence has on student juvenile court exposure have been highly researched and discussed over the past 20 years. How police presence intersects with education and juvenile rights in the educational context will be explored in-depth. Basing this chapter in criminological research performed in 2018 by May and colleagues will allow us to unpack the implications of school resource officers and juvenile court referrals (May, Barranco, Stokes, Robertson, & Haynes, 2018). This research was based on a 2013 *New York Times* article titled "With Police in Schools, More Children in Court" (Eckholm, 2013), which explains the increase in criminal charges against children for school misbehavior (Eckholm, 2013). This *New York Times* article, the Justice Policy Institute (2011) report, and the research cited by May et al. (2018) suggest the need for more examination of police in schools and students who are involved in the juvenile justice system as a result of the increase of police in schools.

Policing schools has been justified by the ruling in *New Jersey v. T.L.O.* (1985) discussed in-depth in Chapter 7. This case established that schools have a duty to maintain a safe environment where learning can take place, thus overriding a student's expectation of privacy when school staff has reasonable suspicion that a student is engaged in delinquent or criminal behavior (*New Jersey v. T.L.O.*, 1985). In this case, the assistant vice principal was suspicious of T.L.O selling drugs on-campus after a teacher reported her behavior in the bathroom. The assistant principal searched T.L.O's purse, contacted the police, and provided them with the items that were removed from T.L.O.'s purse. The police contacted T.L.O.'s mother, and the mother brought her to the police station where she confessed to selling marijuana. Using the items found in T.L.O.'s purse and the confession that she provided to the police, delinquency charges were filed against her. This case, along with the Safe Schools Act of 1994 and the establishment of the Community Oriented Policing Services Office, has justified the continued presence of law enforcement officers in the school environment.

As a rule, officers need probable cause to arrest juveniles, the same as adults. In U.S. criminal law, probable cause is the standard by which an officer or an agent of the law has the grounds to make an arrest, to conduct a personal or property search, or to obtain a warrant for arrest, etc. when criminal charges are being considered. It is also used to refer to the standard to which a grand jury believes that a crime has been committed. This term comes from the Fourth Amendment of the United States Constitution:

"The right of the people to be secure in their persons, houses, papers, and effects, against unreasonable searches and seizures, shall not be violated, and no warrants shall issue, but upon probable cause, supported by Oath or affirmation, and particularly describing the place to be searched, and the persons or things to be seized." "Probable" in this case may relate to actual statistical probability, or to a general standard of common behavior and customs. The context of the word "probable" here is not exclusive to community standards and does not predate statistics, as some have suggested.

The best-known definition of probable cause is "a reasonable belief that a person has committed a crime" (Kinports, 2008). Another common definition is "a reasonable amount of suspicion, supported by circumstances sufficiently strong to justify a prudent and cautious person's belief that certain facts are probably true" (Kinports, 2008). Notable in this definition is a lack of requirement for a public position or public authority of the individual making the recognition, allowing for use of the term by citizens and/or the general public.

In the context of warrants, the *Oxford Companion to American Law* defines probable cause as "information sufficient to warrant a prudent person's belief that the wanted individual had committed a crime (for an arrest warrant) or that evidence of a crime or contraband would be found in a search (for a search warrant)" (Bernhardt, 2002). "Probable cause" is a stronger standard of evidence than a reasonable suspicion, but it is weaker than what is required to secure a criminal conviction. Even hearsay can supply probable cause if it is from a reliable source or supported by other evidence, according to the Aguilar–Spinelli test (Woollcott, 1984).

One key issue around the arrest of juveniles in school settings is the interrogation of students. Before an interrogation of students is permissible and the information obtained from the said interrogation is admissible, *the totality of the circumstance* must be considered. The *totality of the circumstances* standard suggests that there is no single deciding factor; one must consider all the facts and context and conclude from the whole picture whether there is probable cause, or whether an alleged detention is really a detention, or whether a citizen acted under color of law. The primary guide for this kind of substantive rule is the fact patterns from cases in which the courts have found that the criteria were met.

A test originally formulated to evaluate whether a student's individual and constitutional rights were violated during interrogation was previously used. It concentrates on looking at all the circumstances surrounding the alleged violation, rather than only one or two aspects, as had been the case before. It had been used as a measure of whether a defendant's privilege against self-incrimination had been violated, but since the advent of the Miranda rule (1966) that use has become obsolete. It is now used to determine whether a defendant consented to a warrantless search, and whether probable cause exists for the issuing of a search warrant.

In *Miranda v. Arizona* (1966), Ernesto Miranda had been arrested and was in the custody of the Phoenix Police Department for kidnap and rape. He was identified by the key witness and was interrogated for two hours without being notified of his rights to have an attorney present. The police produced a signed confession. At trial, the oral and written confessions were presented to the jury. Miranda was found guilty of kidnapping and rape and was sentenced to 20–30 years' imprisonment on each count. On appeal, the Supreme Court of Arizona held that Miranda's constitutional rights were not violated in obtaining the confession. The U.S. Supreme court held in its decision that:

> defendant's interrogation violated the Fifth Amendment. To protect the privilege, the Court reasoned, procedural safeguards were required. A defendant was required to be warned before questioning that he had the right to remain silent, and that anything he said can be used against him in a court of law. A defendant was required to be told that he had the right to an attorney, and if he could not afford an attorney, one was to be appointed for him prior to any questioning if he so desired. After these warnings were given, a defendant could knowingly and intelligently waive these rights and agree to answer questions or make a statement. Evidence obtained as a result of interrogation was not to be used against a defendant at trial unless the prosecution demonstrated the warnings were given, and knowingly and intelligently waived. (p. 79)

The court clearly advised that adults cannot be held or questioned for long periods of time without being advised of their rights to an attorney to protect against self-incrimination, and safeguard Fifth Amendment rights. The Miranda ruling gave way to court address juvenile confessions in the case of *Fare v. Michael C.* (1979).

In *Fare v. Michael C.* (1979), the court cited age; past police contact or experiences; juvenile court involvement; and the youth's intelligence as determining factors for an interrogation. All these factors plus proper police work is considered in the *totality of the circumstance* for juvenile confessions. Legislation passed in the 1990s has provided law enforcement more access to juveniles in school, making probable cause, totality of the circumstance, and Miranda and Fare rulings more relevant in schools.

The Safe Schools Act of 1994 was passed by the U.S. 103rd Congress as HR Bill 2455. The legislation accomplishes the following:

1. Directs the secretary of education to make competitive grants to eligible local educational agencies for projects to achieve National Education Goal six by helping to ensure that all schools are safe and free of violence.
2. Directs the secretary to develop a written safe schools model.
3. Authorizes appropriations.
4. Authorizes the secretary to use certain reserved funds to conduct national leadership activities, such as research, program development and evaluation, data collection, public awareness activities, training and technical assistance, peer review of applications, and grants for public television video projects for conflict resolution.

Essentially, the Gun-Free Schools Act of 1994 was an amendment to the Elementary and Secondary Education Act of 1965, which funded local education agencies (LEA), primarily public schools that receive federal education assistance, to have in effect a "zero-tolerance" policy (CRS, 2002). "This policy required the expulsion from school for at least one year of any student who brought a gun, knife, or another type of weapon to school. Another key piece of legislation, the Safe Schools Act of 1994, directed the Secretary of Education to make competitive grants to eligible LEAs for projects aimed at ensuring that all schools are safe and free of violence" (Kriger, 2017).

Let's examine the entry and increase of law enforcement officers in schools. McKenna and Pollock (2014) shared the history of police in schools. Their research shows that the first account of law enforcement presence in schools in the United States was in the 1950s in Flint, Michigan (Coon & Travis, 2012). The officer was employed by the City of Flint Police Department but was assigned to work in the school full-time. The main function of school-based officers was identified as reducing crime and delinquency among schoolchildren.

SCHOOL RESOURCE OFFICERS

According to the National Association of School Resource Officers (NASRO), "A school resource officer, by federal definition, is a career law enforcement officer with sworn authority who is deployed by an employing police department or agency in a community-oriented policing assignment to work in collaboration with one or more schools" (NASRO, 2019). NASRO offers training for school resource officers, recommends 40 hours of training, and suggests that states should enforce the rights of these officers to be armed at all times while on duty in schools. As an organization that exists to support school resource officers in schools, the NASRO addresses the school-to-prison pipeline but denounces the idea that the presence of school resource officers in schools shares any culpability in the growth of the pipeline (NASRO, 2019).

Research on the history of school resource officers shows some cases of police operating in schools dating back to 80 years ago, with the Indianapolis Public School Police being reported in 1939, and in 1948, the Los Angeles School Police Department was created as a security section for the school district, while the actual concept of the "school resource officer" originated during the 1950s in Flint, Michigan (Brown, 2006; Monterastelli, 2017). Other reports suggest that it was a chief of police in Miami, Florida, who first used the term in the 1960s as these programs initially began to spread and develop across the country (Lynch, Gainey, & Chappell, 2016).

However, it was only more recently, during the 1990s, that the number of school resource officers and a strong police presence in schools really began to expand. This was seen as a direct response to an overwhelming sense of concern voiced by politicians and citizens regarding their fear of violent crime in schools coupled with a high priority on the enforcement of zero-tolerance policies in schools related to drug and weapon violations. This era also brought along federal dollars, through the Department of Justice and the Department of Education, to support state school initiatives in enforcing zero-tolerance policies through strict policing and enforcement in schools and provided funding for officers, military equipment and tactical gear, and metal detectors, as well as other security devices (Lynch et al., 2016; Peak, 2015).

The continued growth of school police departments across the country is evident by the number of officers now serving as school resource officers. The NASRO estimates that there are anywhere from 14,000 to 20,000 school resource officers currently in schools, but they note that the last official statistics reported by the Department of Justice offered an estimate closer to 17,000 (Trump, 2002). Some schools work with a limited number of resource officers; however, in other districts, the number of school resource officers is quite substantial. For instance, in the Los Angeles School Police Department, there are more than 300 officers who serve in a variety of positions within the schools (Brown, 2006), and in New York City, the security division for their public school system is actually so large that if it were considered a police department, it would rank as the fifth-largest police force in the United States (Peak, 2015). In addition, schools also employ security guards, security personnel, or sworn law enforcement officers who are not school resource officers. During the 2013–2014 school years, the number of personnel serving in all of these different capacities related to school security, including school resource officers, equaled approximately 85,000 employees working across the United States (Ryan et al., 2018).

THE RESPONSIBILITIES AND REALITIES OF SCHOOL RESOURCE OFFICERS

According to the NASRO, "the goals of well-founded SRO programs include providing safe learning environments in our nation's schools, providing valuable resources to school staff members, fostering positive relationships with youth, developing strategies to resolve problems affecting youth and protecting all students, so that they can reach their fullest potentials." The organization suggests that the three main roles of the school resource officer include the primary role of law enforcement officer, informal counselor and/or mentor, and guest lecturer or educator within the schools (NASRO, 2019).

The main duties of school resource officers may often be in law enforcement efforts, including controlling disruptive students, maintaining order within the school, providing regular patrol of school grounds and conducting traffic supervision. In addition, they can actually become involved in a wide variety of activities, such as attending meetings with families and faculty, conducting presentations on-campus for both faculty and students, maintaining a presence at community or school-board meetings, attending parent-teacher conferences, attending off-campus events, and working toward prevention efforts (Brown, 2006). Although, in reality, there are many other types of activities that school resource officers may become involved with while on the job.

While the use of resource officers in schools continues to grow, there are many criticisms about their effectiveness in preventing violence and crime in schools and the role they play in the growth of the school-to-prison pipeline. Abudu and Miles (2017) argued, "While parents and teachers are key stakeholders in advancing a child's educational opportunities, law enforcement and the imposition of adult-like criminal penalties on children are having an opposite, destructive effect" (p. 59).

Research shows that the characteristics of the school where the school resource officer works greatly influence the type of work they are typically engaged in on a day-to-day basis. A recent study examining the effect of educational and social disadvantage in schools on the role school resource officers engage in within schools finds support for this idea. The research found that those school resource officers who were assigned to the schools with the highest level of disadvantage were more likely to be engaged in a high level of law enforcement activities. In addition, they were less likely to be engaged in education and other functions on-campus, and the combined effect of these factors could add support for the conclusion that, especially in disadvantaged schools, school resource officers could be a contributing force to the school-to-prison pipeline (Lynch et al., 2016).

Theriot (2009) found that schools with higher levels of economic disadvantage had a significantly higher rate of arrests overall and specifically for assault, weapons, and disorderly conduct, while the most significant difference was in the rates of arrest for disorderly conduct. As the research pointed out, disorderly conduct is the most subjective offense; it is a product of both situational and circumstantial factors that can, both directly and indirectly, provide an avenue for the disproportionate rate of referrals for exclusionary discipline and arrests of minority students in schools.

It is also important to note that it is not just the school resource officers who may be widening the net of the school-to-prison pipeline in schools. Research shows that schools themselves, parents, and family members, as well as community members, victims, law enforcement outside of schools, and Department of Health Services (DHS) all contribute to the pipeline through the overuse of referring juveniles to the system for minor status offenses (May et al., 2018). One issue involved in how school resource officers operate and their decision-making behaviors in school disciplinary practices in schools can be tied to their level of training. One study found that school resource officers who reported receiving no training were more likely to be primarily involved in law enforcement efforts on the job, while those officers who reported that they wanted higher levels of specialized training were more likely to engage in counseling interventions, along with law enforcement efforts (Martinez-Prather, McKenna, & Bowman, 2016).

The training of school resource officers is imperative in their ability to be a positive influence on school campuses. Research has shown support for training school resource officers in connecting at-risk students with needed services in trauma-informed approaches, and these practices could actually be a positive step in the direction of dismantling the school-to-prison pipeline (Gill, Gottfredson, & Hutzell, 2016). To be effective, school resource officers must build connections with students, providing opportunities for establishing bonds and building positive relationships in schools.

In a recent study, Theriot (2013) found that students who have engaged in interactions with resource officers often have more favorable attitudes toward the officers, yet these students are also most likely to report the lowest level of school connectedness, less likely to

WHAT EFFECTS DO SCHOOL RESOURCE OFFICERS HAVE ON SCHOOLS?

By Richard R. Johnson, PhD (October 2016)

Please click on this hyperlink to access the article:

https://www.dolanconsultinggroup.com/wp-content/uploads/2019/02/What-Effects-do-School-Resource-Officers-Have-on-Schools.pdf

Or scan the QR code with your cell phone to view the article:

report feeling safe at school, and more likely to experience school as a dangerous place. These findings suggest a complex relationship between the roles that resource officers play and the realities of the perceptions and experiences of students. Research offers several suggestions for the successful integration of school resource officers: specifically, extensive training for school resource officers; frequent communication and meetings between school resource officers, teachers, and school administrators; and formal governance documents created to specifically address the responsibilities of school resource officers, teachers, and administrator roles in school discipline. These suggestions can all work to support the success of school resource officers. In conjunction with creating a safe and respectful space, using both positive and non-threatening communication, implementing these changes can reshape the overall school environment and begin to dismantle the school-to-prison pipeline (Theriot & Cuellar, 2016).

HISTORY OF POLICING JUVENILES

The 1950s was a period characterized by the development of professional standards for handling juveniles. In 1955, the formation of the Central States Juvenile Officers Association highlighted the importance of juvenile officers in police departments around the country (Bartollas & Miller, 2005). This organization along with the International Juvenile Officers Association established professional standards in policing juveniles. The 1960s and 1970s provided financial support to the efforts of the 1950s through the creation of the Law Enforcement Assistance Administration (LEAA). This administration provided federal funding to new programs that targeted youth. Police diversion programs steered youth away from formal juvenile justice processing. LEAA provided federal funding for a variety of policing initiatives. For example, diversion programs that provided youth and their families counseling, recreational programs, social skills building, and parenting skills (Roberts, 1989). Other youth programs were developed during the 1950s, such as leadership and moral training, job assistance, and programs intended to reduce truancy (Bartollas & Miller, 2005).

CONTEMPORARY POLICING OF JUVENILES

The 1970s and 1980s were characterized by budget cuts, which resulted in the reduction or elimination of specialized juvenile units. These decades focused primarily on family violence and gang programs. Gangs were extremely problematic for police, especially in large jurisdictions. There was an increase in the attention on juvenile delinquency during the 1980s and 1990s due to the increase in youth violence during this period. The 1990s once again focused more attention on youths due to the increased concerns over juvenile crime. Clearly, police have considerable power and responsibility and they perform numerous duties policing juveniles. However, does this make them equipped to police schools? Psychologically, police have attitudes and beliefs about what people think about policing. This is important because the police and the pubic have expectations about police work and performance. Take, for example, the 2015 incident of the Black female student in South Carolina (Fedders, 2016) who experienced use of force by a South Carolina deputy sheriff for refusing to leave the classroom when requested by her teacher. Most who saw the video footage of the incident (https://www.youtube.com/watch?v=qBSrccdaqXo) thought it was use of excessive force by the school resource officer to remove the student from her seat. The contemporary role of police is complex and often characterized by conflict, which leads scholars, teachers, and parents to speculate the effectiveness of police in schools. With all that is going on with police brutality, some parents and guardians dislike the idea of having armed police used as resource officers in a place where their children are learning.

Police serve three basic functions: law enforcement, order maintenance, and service (Wilson, 1978). Today's police have a role to enforce the law through detection, apprehension, and prevention of illegal behavior. The presence of police in schools poses some challenges to the educational environment, since a primary responsibility is collecting evidence that can be used in the prosecution of cases. Police enforce legal statutes including traffic, juvenile, and criminal codes; investigating crimes; chasing and arresting suspects; and transporting suspects to jail. A shift in roles often causes police to experience police role conflict influenced by their different responsibilities. Police are expected to prevent crime and respond to illegal behavior of juveniles, but/ and they are also expected to protect the rights of everyone in the school environment. This expectation can be counterproductive for schools. Many police recognize that the arrest of a student for minor illegal behavior, such as a school yard fight, might result in more harm than good and could be better handled in an informal manner. However, zero-tolerance policies dictate otherwise.

Police in schools encounter students under stressful conditions. School police play an important role in shaping the attitudes that police and juvenile share. It is vitally important that school police are carefully trained in responding to youth. One approach has involved training individual officers assigned to schools in how to approach juveniles. Officers in small departments may receive less training in dealing with juveniles, because they typically have less resources. Another approach involves developing specialized units to handle more serious juvenile cases, like that in 1980s and 1990s. Factors that influence police decisions to arrest juveniles should include seriousness of the offense; the assigning police organization (why public schools have an independent police department) policies and culture; community and resources available to respond to youthful behavior; wishes of the complainants; demeanor and presentation of youth; gender; race; and social class. Officers from more legalistic departments are more likely to arrest juvenile suspects on or off-campus than those from less legalistic departments (Smith, 1984). For example, in one community only 9% of students who had contact with police were referred to court, in another community 71% were referred for juvenile court processing (Goldman, 1963).

The variability in how police departments respond to juvenile delinquents is partially the product of the differences in department organizational characteristics and their policies, procedures, and culture. Community attitudes and characteristics influence both departmental and individual police officer's response to juvenile delinquency. Communities that have programs that handle juveniles provide officers with resources. Officers who have resources such as conflict resolution or victim restitutions programs are less likely to arrest. Some communities just do not have these resources available for the officers who police juveniles.

When police prevent youth from engaging in delinquent activity, they spare youth the stigma associated with formal juvenile court processing. Prevention also spares the court time and cost associated with processing cases and allows the juvenile legal system more time to focus on serious offenses. Drug abuse resistance education (DARE) was the most widely used school-based prevention program, and is operational even today with private funding, although it has lost its popularity. DARE used uniformed officers to present a structured curriculum designed to help students avoid drugs, violence, and peer pressure. This program operated in 75% of the nation's schools and in more than 43 countries around the world based on its claims of successfulness; however, after numerous evaluations of several versions of DARE, the results suggested otherwise (Sorenson, 2012). The research indicated that exposure to the DARE program resulted in increased attitudes and knowledge about drugs and perceptions of the police, but this increase in knowledge quickly dissipated.

Gang Resistance Education and Training (GREAT), another school-based prevention program like DARE, consists of a curriculum taught by police officers in elementary and middle schools in almost every state. Over the years GREAT has made its curriculum more interactive to promote the relationship between gangs and violence. The interactive format helps foster an understanding about what can be done about gangs, goal setting, social competencies development, and communication and conflict resolution skills (Esbensen, Freng, Taylor, Peterson, & Osgood, 2002). GREAT has had positive evaluations, although the primary goal to prevent youth gang participation has not been achieved. Nonetheless, students gain prosocial attitudes, display less risky behavior, are victimized less, and develop less favorable attitudes toward gangs (Esbensen et al., 2002).

Community policing is another strategy used to work with the local community to identify and understand the social context of delinquency and rectify the problems caused by delinquent behavior (Trojanowicz & Bucqueroux, 1998). Youth-oriented community policing programs have multiple goals:

1. To provide a multiagency response to children and their families in order to prevent future delinquent behavior and adult criminality.
2. To work with youth who are already involved with the juvenile courts to reduce the likelihood of recidivism.
3. To develop closer relations between community residents, public officials, and the police.

Cooperative multi-agency teams address communities' problems. The multi-agency teams are usually staffed by mental health agency representatives, school officials, social service agencies, health departments, colleges and universities, and neighborhood associations, just to name a few (Cohn, 1996). The focus is on the social context in which delinquency takes place. This approach allows law enforcement to identify the social factors related to delinquency and take positive actions to address these factors in order to prevent delinquency.

POLICING SCHOOLS IMPLICATIONS ON JUVENILE JUSTICE

When police work with and not against educators, parents, and community groups, evidence suggests that they can play an important role in meeting the social justice needs of youth in the community and form strong police–school partnerships (Brady, Balmer, & Phenix, 2007). However, police in schools can result in the criminalization of behavior that was previously handled by effective school policies, not the formal juvenile justice process. Consider a 6-year-old student who hits a school official (commits a felony—assault) and resists arrest (a misdemeanor) and throws a tantrum (another misdemeanor) (Price, 2008). Should this 6-year-old student be arrested? Desree Watson, a 6-year-old first grader in Florida, was arrested, taken to the juvenile detention facility, fingerprinted, and charged with felony battery for assaulting a school official and two misdemeanors for resisting arrest and disorderly conduct (Herbert, 2007). The tendency to criminalize childhood behavior is more common than many believe. Look at Dallas, Texas, and other cities in Texas where police officers use class "C" misdemeanors in citations for status offenses such as truancy and other violations of school-based policies such as dress code and classroom disruption. More than one in seven students in Texas have been involved with the juvenile justice system. Students who are detained as a result of contact with juvenile courts are three times more likely to end up in adult prisons (Robinson & Aronica, 2016).

"Booking Students: An Analysis of School Arrests and Court Outcomes" published in the *Northwestern Journal of Law and Social Policy* (Wolf, 2013) provides a comprehensive picture of the implications that policing schools have on juvenile court processing. It provides a profile of school arrests that aims to improve our understanding of the students who are arrested, the charges they face, and the outcomes of their delinquency proceedings. The article shows that police most often arrest students for relatively minor misbehaviors, with misdemeanors comprising more than 90% of lead charges against arrested students. It also shows how black students are 3 times more likely to be arrested than their white peers. This remarkably disproportionate rate reinforces the information provided in Chapter 4.

Wolf's (2013) analysis of school arrests and court outcomes reviewed how police tend to employ arrests differently to control the behavior of female students. The data on school arrests indicates that the police are more apt to use arrests as a response when females fight or otherwise act disorderly, another point expounding on in Chapter 4. Policing school data demonstrates that black females were two times more likely to be arrested for fighting than white males, even though black girls were a smaller percentage of the student population. Lastly, a large number of arrests are dismissed in lieu of delinquency adjudications for white students, with the dismissals stemming from community service or diversion programs. This suggests that there is a large number of arrests of minority students whose misbehavior will result in court processing from in-school disciplinary matters.

DISCUSSION QUESTIONS

1. How did police presence start in schools?
2. What is the significance of the Safe School Act of 1994?
3. How did the Gun-Free Schools Act of 1994 affect education agencies?
4. What were the strategies for implementing school resource officers into the educational environment?

REFERENCES

Abudu, N. & Miles, R. (2017). Challenging the status quo: An integrated approach to dismantling the school-to-prison pipeline. *St. Thomas Law Review, 30,* 56–67.

Bartollas, C., & Miller, S. J. (2005). *Juvenile justice in America* (4th ed.). Upper Saddle River, NJ: Pearson Prentice Hall.

Bernhardt, R. (2002). *The Oxford companion to American law.* Oxford: Oxford University Press.

Brady, K. P., Balmer, S., & Phenix, D. (2007). School–police partnership effectiveness in urban schools: An analysis of New York City's impact schools initiative. *Education and Urban Society, 39*(4), 455–478.

Brown, B. (2006). Understanding and assessing school police officers: A conceptual and methodological comment. *Journal of Criminal Justice, 34*, 591–604. Doi:10.1016/j.jcrimjus.2006.09.013

Cohn, E. G. (1996). The citizen police academy: A recipe for improving police-community relations. *Journal of Criminal Justice, 24*(3), 265–271.

Coon, J., & Travis, L. (2012). The role of police in public schools: A comparison of police and principal reports of activities in schools. *Police Practice and Research: An International Journal, 13*(1), 15–30.

CRS. (2002). *The Safe and Drug-Free Schools and Communities Act: Reauthorization and appropriations,* (CRS Report for Congress RS20532), 26–27, Washington, DC: Library of Congress. Retrieved from https://digital.library.unt.edu/ark:/67531/metacrs2209/m1/1/high_res_d/RS20532_2002Aug01.pdf

Eckholm, E. (2013). With police in schools, more children in court. *New York Times*, A1.

Esbensen, F. A., Freng, A., Taylor, T. J., Peterson, D., & Osgood, D. W. (2002). National evaluation of the gang resistance education and training (G.R.E.A.T.) program. In W. L. Reed & S. H. Decker (Eds.), *Responding to gangs: Evaluation and research* (pp. 139–168). Washington, DC: U.S. Department of Justice.

Fedders, B. (2016). The anti-pipeline collaborative. *Wake Forest Law Review, 51*, 565.

Gill, C., Gottfredson, D., & Hutzell, K. (2016). Can school policing be trauma-informed? Lessons from Seattle. *Policing; Bradford, 39*(3), 551–565.

Goldman, N. (1963). *The differential selection of juvenile offenders for court appearance.* New York, NY: National Research and Information Center, National Council on Crime and Delinquency.

Herbert, B. (2007). 6-Year-olds under arrest. *New York Times.* pp. A17, Op-Ed 9.Retrieved from https://www.nytimes.com/2007/04/09/opinion/09herbert.html

Justice Policy Institute. (2011). *Education under arrest: The case against police in schools.* Retrieved from http://www.justicepolicy.org/uploads/justicepolicy/documents/educationunderarrest_fullreport.pdf

Kinports, K. (2008). Diminishing probable cause and minimalist searches. *Ohio State Journal of Criminal Law, 6*, 649–660.

Kriger, N. (2017). *School safety policies and programs administered by the US federal government: 1990-2016.*

Lynch, C., Gainey, R., & Chappell, A. (2016). The effects of social and educational disadvantage on the roles and functions of school resource officers. *Policing; Bradford, 39*(3), 521–535.

Martinez-Prather, K., McKenna, J., & Bowman, S., (2016). The impact of training on discipline outcomes in school-based policing. *Policing; Bradford, 39*(3), 478–490.

May, D. C., Barranco, R., Stokes, E., Robertson, A. A., & Haynes, S. H. (2018). Do school resource officers really refer juveniles to the juvenile justice system for less serious offenses? *Criminal Justice Policy Review, 29*(1) 89–105. doi: 10.1177/0887403415610167

McKenna, J. M. & Pollock, J. M. (2014). Law enforcement officers in school: An analysis of ethical issues. *Criminal Justice Ethics*, *33*, 163–184.

Miranda v. Arizona, 384 U.S. 436 (1966)

Monterastelli, S. (2017). Every hand's a loser: The intersection of zero-tolerance policies, mental illness in children and adolescents, and the juvenile justice system. *Law & Psychology Review*, *41*, 209–228.

National Association of School Resource Officers (NASRO). (2019). Frequently asked questions. Retrieved from: https://nasro.org/frequently-asked-questions/

New Jersey v. T.L.O., 469 U.S. 325 (1985).

Peak, B. (2015). Militarization of school police: One route on the school-to-prison pipeline. *Arkansas Law Review*, *68*, 195–229.

Price, P. (2008). When is a police officer an officer of the law: The status of police officers in schools. *Journal of Criminal Law & Criminology*, *99*, 541.

Roberts, A. R., & MacHardy, L. W. (1989). *Juvenile justice: Policies, programs, and services.* Chicago, IL: Dorsey Press.

Robinson, K., & Aronica, L. (2016). *Creative schools: The grassroots revolution that's transforming education.* New York, NY: Penguin Books.

Ryan, J. B., Katsiyannis, A., Counts, J. M., & Shelnut, J. C. (2018). The growing concerns regarding school resource officers. *Intervention in School and Clinic*, *53*(3), 188–192.

Smith, D. A. (1984). The organizational context of legal control. *Criminology*, *22*(1), 19–38.

Sorenson, J. E. (2012, Spring/Summer). *DARE Newsletter*, *15*, 2/3.

Theriot, M. (2009). School resource officers and the criminalization of student behavior. *Journal of Criminal Justice*, *37*(3), 280–287.

Theriot, M. (2013). The impact of school resource officer interaction on students' feelings about school and school police. *Crime & Delinquency*, *62*(4), 446–469.

Theriot, M., & Cuellar, M. (2016). School resource officers and students' rights. *Contemporary Justice Review*, *19*(3), 363–379

Trojanowicz, R. C., & Bucqueroux, B. (1998). *Community policing: How to get started.* New York, NY: Routledge.

Trump, K. S. (2002). NASRO School Resource Officer Survey, 2002: Final Report on the *2nd Annual National Survey of School-Based Police Officers.*

Wilson, J. Q. (1978). *Varieties of police behavior: The management of law and order in eight communities, with a new preface by the author.* Boston, MA: Harvard University Press.

Wolf, K. C. (2013). Booking students: An analysis of school arrests and court outcomes. *Northwestern University Journal of Law and Social Policy*, *9*, i.

(2013, April 12). With police in schools, more children in court. *The New York Times*, p. A1. Retrieved from http://www.nytimes.com/2013/04/12/education/with-police-in-schools-more-children-in-court.html?pagewanted=all

Woollcott, A. P. (1984). Abandonment of the two-pronged Aguilar-Spinelli test Illinois v. Gates. *Cornell Law Review*, *70*, 316.

CHAPTER SIX

Post-Arrest Proceeding and Educational Implications

Georgen Guerrero

READING OBJECTIVES

- Understand the basic referral procedures for law enforcement, intake probation officers, and juvenile court judges.
- Define various terms that are used in the juvenile justice system.
- Identify the basic educational options available to juveniles in the juvenile justice system.
- Summarize the efforts of criminal justice personnel in processing juveniles and the court's efforts to educate juveniles.

OVERVIEW

There are a multitude of pathways for a juvenile once the youth has been taken into custody and referred to the juvenile justice system. While most juveniles will be released back into society by various participants in the juvenile system, there are a small handful who will not get released. As education is strongly associated with reduced recidivism (Herz et al., 2012), those juveniles who do not get released back into society will have numerous educational opportunities afforded to them. These programs are delivered to the incarcerated with the understanding that an individual who is given the opportunity to complete an educational program is more likely to avoid future delinquent and criminal behavior (Herz et al., 2012). Typically, juveniles who are incarcerated will have greater educational needs than juveniles who are not incarcerated (Weissman et al., 2008) because of lower completion rates, a history of failure, and being retained at least once (Foley, 2001).

LAW ENFORCEMENT AND JUVENILE PROCESSING CENTERS

As schools increased the number of zero-tolerance policies, they also increased the number of law enforcement personnel on their campuses (National Research Council, 2013). As the number of law enforcement officers hired to patrol school hallways and intervene in disciplinary issues at schools has increased, there has also been an increase in the number of juveniles who have been taken into custody (Weissman et al., 2008), despite the fact that overall, juvenile delinquency has been declining (Snyder & Sickmund, 2006). Once a juvenile has been taken into custody by a law enforcement officer for a delinquent act, the juvenile will be escorted to a local processing facility. Police are the main source of referrals to local juvenile departments; however, juveniles can be referred by parents, schools, and social service agents (Snyder & Sickmund, 2006).

Many jurisdictions have local *processing centers* at respective schools or at a small number of schools within the school district. These processing centers can take on many forms but are usually small, isolated offices that are kept sight-and-sound separated from the rest of the general school population. Depending on schools' resources, these processing centers can be very elaborate, filled with high-tech security equipment, or very basic, such as a small portable undecorated mini-storage-sized room.

These small individualized processing centers are merely locations where law enforcement officers are able to take the juvenile into custody, fingerprint the juvenile, photograph the juvenile, and complete any other necessary paperwork to refer the matter to the juvenile court. These processing centers may be viewed as minisubstations for local independent school district officers, the local police department, or even campus security to be housed or to conduct their daily school-related security business. These processing centers may have additional security equipment or staff working in them. School districts that equip their campuses with security cameras may use these processing centers to house these cameras, thus allowing officers to review any security footage before, after, or during an alleged event for their police reports.

Whenever a law enforcement officer takes a juvenile into custody, the officer will decide what to do with the juvenile. The law enforcement officer primarily has two options at this stage. The officer can release the juvenile back into the custody of his legal guardians or can take the juvenile to the local juvenile department to be handed over to a juvenile probation officer who will complete the intake process for the prosecuting office.

The law enforcement officer will decide how to continue the processing of a juvenile through a range of threat and risk factors. However, the primary threat and risk factors that may influence a law enforcement officer's decision include the seriousness of the charge, prior history of arrest, likelihood of absconding, level of threat the juvenile poses to society and self, and whether a weapon was used in the commission of the offense. If an officer assesses these factors and finds that the juvenile with a long history of committing delinquent acts is alleged to have committed a serious offense with a weapon and has a high probability of reoffending or absconding, it would be in the best interest of everyone involved that the juvenile be taken to the local juvenile probation department.

In addition to the child's threat and risk levels, there are other factors that may assist an officer in deciding how to process a juvenile through the juvenile justice system. The size of the law enforcement agency, the location of the school or school district in relation to the juvenile department, or even the availability of the legal guardians can have some influence on this decision. If the agency does not have an officer who is readily available to transport the juvenile to the juvenile department, or the juvenile department is multiple cities (but in the same county) away, then the officer may seek alternative options rather than transporting the juvenile to the juvenile department. In addition, if the parents are present, as they routinely are in school settings, the officer may decide to release the child to the parents after the initial processing.

If the juvenile poses a minimal risk to others in society, to self, and to the legal system through chances of absconding or recidivating, the officer may release the juvenile back into the custody of his or her parents. Once the juvenile is returned to the custody of the legal guardian, the officer will simply refer all necessary paperwork to the local juvenile department to follow up with the juvenile and his or her family on a later date. The juvenile is in essence released into the custody of his or her parents on the child's own (or guardian's) recognizance. It will be the parents' responsibility to return the juvenile to the juvenile court or the local juvenile department when requested. However, the arresting officer has no obligation to release the juvenile back into the custody of his or her parents. At this stage in the proceeding, it is up to the arresting officer to decide what the initial outcome will be for the juvenile. Despite the fact that many jurisdictions offer law enforcement officers the option of releasing juveniles back into the custody of their legal guardians, most officers will simply take a juvenile into custody, take him or her to the juvenile department to complete the formalization process (complete all necessary paperwork, fingerprints, photographs, etc.), and then release him or her into the custody of a juvenile probation officer.

THE JUVENILE PROBATION OFFICER

The juvenile probation officer, who has quite a bit of discretion in the matter, will examine the necessary paperwork to receive the juvenile from the officer. The juvenile probation officer, also known as an intake probation officer, will be examining several items depending on the jurisdiction, including ensuring that the individual in custody is, in fact, a juvenile, in accordance with his or her respective jurisdictions (legal juvenile ages differ from state to state) and ensuring that the arresting officer has clearly articulated the *probable cause* needed to make the arrest, completed all arresting paperwork, and properly fingerprinted and photographed the juvenile, if required, as each state will have different requirements.

Once the intake probation officer has completed the initial screening of the necessary referral paperwork, he or she, or some other juvenile officer, will conduct an institutional in-custody *pat search* of the juvenile to ensure that he or she is not bringing any type of drugs or weapons into the juvenile facility. Despite the fact that nearly all juveniles will be pat searched by law enforcement officers when they are taken into custody, they will be pat searched again once they arrive at the local juvenile facility for the protection of the juvenile, other juveniles at the facility, and the juvenile staff working at the facility.

It is unlikely that these follow-up pat searches will produce any undiscovered drugs or weapons, but on occasion, it does occur. If there are any drugs or weapons found on the juvenile during this pat search, the arresting officer will have the discretion of filing additional charges on the juvenile for being in possession of illegal drugs or weapons. In most jurisdictions, the bringing of a drug or a weapon into a juvenile facility is classified as an enhanced charge, meaning that the charge will be enhanced by one degree in accordance with the particular state's classification system. For example, in Texas, a juvenile who is in possession of less than 2 ounces of marijuana could be taken into custody and eventually charged with a class B misdemeanor. However, if the same juvenile is in possession of less than 2 ounces of marijuana and brings it into an institutional facility, that juvenile will be charged with a class A misdemeanor—a more serious charge by one degree of enhancement of the original charge.

Once the juvenile has been accepted into the juvenile facility, the probation officer will conduct a preliminary *presentence investigation* (PSI) on the juvenile. The preliminary PSI is a detailed social history on the juvenile that will generally include an inquiry of the juvenile's standing at school and his or her home life, peers, drug and alcohol history, any prior history with the department or other departments, extracurricular activities, work history, and issues or problems that the juvenile is encountering. The juvenile will also undergo various types of preliminary health, drug, or psychological screeners to assist medical or psychological teams with future assessments that will be more in-depth and detailed. The PSI will help the probation officer to determine what actions should be taken with the juvenile.

In the same manner as the referring law enforcement officer, the juvenile probation officer has the discretion to release the juvenile back into the custody of the legal guardian or remain detained at the detention facility. The detention of a juvenile is not intended to be punitive and is avoided if at all possible. However, because of the potential threat to the juvenile or society (Austin, Johnson, & Weitzer, 2005), some juveniles will be detained.

Juveniles do not have a constitutional right to bail as adults do in the criminal justice system; however, they can be released to their parents or guardians without bail if appropriate supervision is available (National Research Council, 2013). If the juvenile is released into the custody of their parents or guardians, then he or she will be released on a type of informal *pretrial probation* with a select number of informal probation rules, such as abide by all laws, do not use any drugs or alcohol, do not leave the jurisdiction without permission, do not skip school, do not associate with negative peers, do not have any contact with the victim, and abide by all house rules. Approximately 45% of juveniles will be diverted through the pretrial alternatives (National Research Council, 2013). Pretrial probation is a court alternative that is usually offered to first-time, low-risk offenders.

This pretrial probation will generally not have any court binding power, but it is used to offer juveniles who have not had any past delinquency issues an opportunity to avoid the court process. If the juvenile does not violate any laws or avoids being re-referred to the department, then the youth will be able to successfully close out the case without having to stand trial. The pretrial rules that are established will help guide and assist the parents in supervising their youth until they are requested to return to the court or the department on a different day. It also assists in alerting the juvenile to the seriousness of the situation and that he or she may have to appear in the presence of a juvenile court judge on a different date. These pretrial probation diversion programs help divert juveniles away from detention and generally last for approximately 3 to 6 months.

INITIAL HEARING WITH A JUVENILE COURT JUDGE

If the juvenile is detained at the juvenile facility, he or she will generally appear for a *probable cause hearing, initial hearing,* or *initial detention hearing* (depending on the state's procedure and terminology) in front of a judge within 24–48 hours (National Research Council, 2013). During the detention hearing, the juvenile court judge will examine the referring paperwork, determine if there is enough probable cause for the officer to have had made the arrest, and determine if the juvenile needs to remain in custody or can be released into the custody of his or her parents. The juvenile's case is constantly being reviewed by several individuals throughout the intake process to ensure that the youth is not being illegally detained and to determine the best possible outcome for the juvenile.

If the juvenile court judge determines that the officer did not have probable cause to make the arrest, then the juvenile will be immediately released from the facility into the custody of his or her guardians, and the alleged charges will be immediately dismissed. As a result of the countless hours of training that law enforcement officers undergo during and after the academy, the likelihood of a law enforcement officer not having probable cause is minimal; however, on occasion, it does occur. An officer may simply not have enough probable cause to have made an arrest; however, at other times, it may actually just be a different interpretation of the offense from the officer to the prosecutor or the judge. There may be a general consensus of the interpretation of the alleged offense at the police department and a completely different interpretation at the prosecuting office or with the judge, causing the charges to be dropped.

As a simple example, an *assault on a public servant* may be interpreted by a police officer as an assault on an officer, a schoolteacher, a firefighter, or anyone who works in the public sector. However, a judge or a prosecutor may interpret that same offense as an assault on law enforcement officers only. There may be a general consensus at the prosecuting office that schoolteachers, firefighters, etc., are not public servants, as they do not have arresting powers. As a result of this particular offense causing some confusion in the criminal and juvenile justice systems, many states have recently passed legislation for a new offense, specifically entitled an *assault on a law enforcement officer* to ensure that there is no confusion about which charge should be applied.

Outside of not having probable cause, if the juvenile court judge determines that the juvenile may be released, then the youth will be released to his or her parents until the juvenile is required to return to court. The juvenile will return to court for *an* arraignment, initial hearing, *or a* pretrial hearing (depending on the state's procedure and terminology), where several legal issues will be resolved, such as an appointment of counsel for the youth, an opportunity for the juvenile to admit or deny the charges that have been presented, or the youth's detention or condition of release status determined pending trial (National Research Council, 2013).

If the juvenile denies the charges by pleading "*not true,*" an *adjudication hearing* may be set in which the juvenile will appear in the presence of the juvenile court judge on a different date and have to stand trial for the alleged offense, and either a judge or a jury will make a determination that the petition was found to be *true* or *not true*. The juvenile system does not use the terminology of guilty or not guilty; a petition brought against a juvenile is found to be true or not true (Texas Lawyers Association, 2018).

A jury may be used if it is allowed in a particular state, as juveniles do not have a constitutional right to jury trials (McKeiver v. Pennsylvania, 1971). The court has many options in considering the handling of a case, and it may decide if it wants to dismiss the case, send the case to prosecution, or offer a voluntary or involuntary probation (National Research Council, 2013). During all of the court hearings, the juvenile is afforded the same access to an attorney as an adult (In re Gault, 1967). However, if the juvenile admits the charges by pleading "*true,*" then the court may move to set a *dispositional hearing.*

If the case is moved to a dispositional hearing or if the court finds the petition to be true, which results in moving to a dispositional hearing, then the judge may impose any number of sanctions on the juvenile. The juvenile court judge has a wide range of options for dealing with the alleged offense and the juvenile when attempting to determine the best possible *disposition* for the juvenile. The judge may decide to place the juvenile on regular probation, informal probation, detention, in residential placement, in a juvenile justice alternative education program (JJAEP), or any number of alternative sanctions. However, these sanctions will always include some type of education-related programs, along with traditional probation regulations, such as restitution, community service, home detention, or curfew restrictions.

EDUCATION-RELATED SANCTIONS

With the understanding that poor school performance is one of the strongest predictors of delinquency (Herrenkohl, Hawkins, Chung, Hill, & Battin-Pearson, 2001; Moffitt, Lynam, & Silva, 1994; Seguin, Pihl, Harden, Tremblay, & Boulerice, 1995), a juvenile court judge has the option to impose on a juvenile a direct order to attend school. The judge can simply mandate that the child remain in school. If the juvenile is found to be in violation of that directive, then the youth can, in most cases will, be taken into custody and returned to the detention facility where the youth will enroll in the school's educational system at the detention center. The juvenile's participation in an educational program while under the direction of the juvenile justice system is imperative, as enrollment in an academic program is strongly associated with lower rates of reoffending (Herz et al., 2012).

In addition, a judge may determine that a general equivalency diploma (GED) may be appropriate for the juvenile depending on a variety of factors, such as age, past academic deficiencies, and the likelihood of completing a traditional educational program. Juvenile court judges will generally invest a great deal of time and energy in trying to assist youth in their courts. If it is determined that a GED will help the juvenile, then it may very well be ordered that the juvenile complete an educational program while incarcerated or on probation. GED programs are found throughout the juvenile justice system. Almost all juvenile programs that offer traditional educational programs, such as detention facilities, residential placements, state commitment centers, and probation departments, will offer juveniles the opportunity to complete a GED program. GED programs are an absolute necessity, as there is a strong correlation between dropping out of school and being involved in the juvenile system (Andrei, Teodorescu, & Oancea, 2012; Kim, 2012). If reenrolling a juvenile into a traditional school is not an option, then a GED program may be a viable solution.

There is very little information available about the quality of education that is generally provided to juveniles who are incarcerated (Weissman et al., 2008). However, in 2014, the Obama administration unveiled its Guiding Principles for Providing High-Quality Education in Juvenile Justice Secure Care Settings, which was implemented to improve the quality of education in secure facilities. The guidelines are driven by five principles: (1) a safe and healthy learning environment, (2) adequate funding, (3) recruitment and retention of qualified educational staff, (4) rigorous and relevant curriculum, and (5) formal processes and procedures that offer a suggestive framework for implementing high-quality education to those incarcerated (U.S. Departments of Education and Justice, 2014). Under the direction of these principles, juvenile facilities are assisted in establishing a foundation for educating youth who are incarcerated.

Detention

Approximately 18,000 juveniles are incarcerated in detention facilities (The Council of State Governments Justice Center, 2015). If detained at the local detention center, the youth will be required to engage in numerous structured detention activities, including being entered into the appropriate grade level through the local school district's educational programming inside the juvenile detention center. The detention center will provide the physical space needed for the teachers and students to operate as close to a normal school setting as possible, with the teachers having classrooms, possibly individual offices or a shared office, and all the normal classroom basic needs, such as desks and chalkboards. The detention facility will also provide an adequate number of staff members to supervise the juveniles while they are in the classrooms interacting with their peers and teachers, while the independent school district will supply the teachers, textbooks, curriculum, and general supplies that are not deemed a safety or security risk. Any item that can break (beakers, microscopes, etc.) or can be used as a weapon will generally not be allowed into a detention facility (McCluskey, 2017).

The local detention center will have a normal academic schedule for the juvenile to follow. The juvenile will have the opportunity to complete all the required coursework for his or her appropriate grade, such as mathematics, science, history, social science, English, recreation, and many other general electives, depending on the agency size and ability to accommodate the school's curriculum and the school district's ability to provide the appropriate number of instructors. Generally speaking, some of these campuses are adequately staffed with an appropriate number of academic instructors and staff for security purposes to maintain a positive learning environment. In addition to academic opportunities, detention centers may offer educational programs to help juveniles address their drug-related problems. Once the juvenile is released from the detention center, all grades and attendance records will be sent to the local school district to record the youth's progress.

The secure structure of the detention atmosphere inside of the classroom setting may allow students to stay focused on their schoolwork with minimal distractions that are usually present at normal schools. Being in a secure environment allows students to arrive on time to classes, minimizes their absences, and keeps them away from the normal school dangers, such as drugs, guns, and alcohol. Student-to-teacher ratios are generally smaller than traditional classroom settings, which helps with the learning environment. In addition, any classroom disruptions are quickly defused by the detention officers who may be present to prevent large-scale problems from erupting. As a result of the structured environment of a detention facility, many times, the juvenile may experience an increase in grade performance, which the youth may not have experienced in a normal educational setting. Furthermore, when the student returns to his or her original school, as a direct result of being able to study in a less distracting environment for even a short period of time, the student is able to get back on track with his or her educational learning at the local school district.

Despite all of the added benefits of the detention atmosphere, there are still other issues that these youth will have to maneuver through a bit more than they may have in traditional school settings, such as being incarcerated with rival gang members, a heightened sense of aggression from other peers, and strict teachers and/or staff. If a juvenile is involved in a disruption, then the youth can be placed in solitary confinement and lose the opportunity to complete coursework for the day (McCluskey, 2017) or even multiple days.

Educational departments at detention centers are unique in that they will have to accommodate multiple juveniles in various grade levels at the same time and usually in the same classrooms. It is very common for a math teacher, for example, to be teaching algebra, geometry, and trigonometry all at the same time in the same classroom to three different students in three different grades. While at the exact same time another teacher will be teaching English I, English II, and English III to three other juveniles in an adjoining classroom. As a result, the teachers will have to be certified to teach at multiple grade levels and teachers with these types of credentials are not often available. In addition, as teachers are getting pulled from one student to the next, a juvenile may receive less instructional time than at the youth's home school (Leone & Weinberg, 2010) outside of the facility.

In addition, to mix up things a little more, these juveniles will generally only be enrolled for very short periods at a time, from as little as one day to on average about 14 days. Therefore, the teachers are constantly having to find the appropriate place to start a student's curriculum upon the youth's arrival. They have very little time to determine the student's learning ability. However, in rare high-profile cases or cases with serious charges, a juvenile may spend a little more time in detention than the average juvenile. The juvenile's constant interruption with the system could also affect the learning environment. It is not uncommon for a juvenile to arrive on Monday on one offense, get released by Wednesday, and then return the following Monday on a new offense. Depending on the seriousness of the charges and the child's preliminary PSI, the juvenile may not stay very long in detention, even on the subsequent referral.

Residential Facilities
When examining the number of referrals that are sent to the juvenile justice system, the probability of a juvenile being placed in a residential facility is relatively low. Residential placements encompass only 9% of all juveniles who are referred to the

juvenile system (National Research Council, 2013). However, if the juvenile is placed in a traditional nonsecure residential facility, then the juvenile may simply have to enroll in a different school or a different school district. However, the advantage of a nonsecure residential placement is that it will routinely allow a juvenile to remain in traditional school settings. The juvenile may even have the advantage of "starting over" at a traditional new school, maybe in a new school district, or in a new town with a clean slate. The youth may have had some peer issues ranging anywhere from peer pressure, to gangs, to drugs, to negative peers, to school administrators. The youth may be able to circumvent old problems at a new school where he or she is unknown to others.

There are a growing number of secure juvenile residential facilities that are being used throughout the United States. In structure, the facilities will look just like secure detention facilities but will be considered postadjudication facilities as opposed to preadjudication facilities. These facilities may operate with the local independent school district in much the same way as detention facilities, with the school district supplying the teachers, textbooks, curriculum, and general supplies for the students at the facility.

The major difference between a secure residential facility and a detention facility is that a juvenile will generally stay for a longer period of time in a residential facility when compared to a detention facility. An average length of stay for a residential facility is anywhere from 6 to 9 months, while a detention center will generally be only for 10 to 14 days. However, many times a 6- to 9-month sentence may result in a longer 12- to 18-month stay. This extension may be a result of a juvenile not complying with the program's rules, thus extending the original sentence. However, on the flip side, a program that is working may be seen as a great alternative to the juvenile's home or school life, and it may be determined that the juvenile remaining at the residential facility until a later date is in the best interest of the child.

In terms of educational potential, the long-term philosophy of a secure residential facility will generally benefit the juvenile a little more than a short-term detention stay. The instructor is able to learn the juvenile's learning style and academic strengths and weaknesses, as well as monitor long-term progress. The juvenile is not being bounced back and forth from the home school, to the detention center, and back to the home school as when he or she is being repeatedly referred to a detention center on new offenses or violations of his or her probation.

Juvenile Justice Alternative Education Programs (JAEPs)

JJAEPs are another option for juveniles who have come in contact with the juvenile justice system. Alternative education programs, such as JJAEPs, are generally reserved for students who have been dismissed from the local school district for violating some law that may be harmful or disruptive to the school (Cortez, 1999), such as the unlawful carrying of a weapon on school grounds. The juvenile has not only violated school policy but also broken the law. Consequently, the juvenile is removed from the school setting through a dismissal or expulsion, while at the same time the youth is referred to the juvenile justice system for the violation of law. In removing the juvenile from the school setting, the juvenile justice system does not remove the youth from the school system, just from the traditional school setting.

JJAEPs were designed to prevent the loss of juveniles to the streets once they are dismissed from their local school districts (Cortez, 1999). The goal of a JJAEP is to increase offender accountability and to rehabilitate offenders through a community-based educational probation system. By giving juveniles an alternative location to complete their education, the juvenile justice system may be helping a very large number of juveniles avoid a multitude of problems, such as not graduating from school, becoming jobless in the future, not having job potential, homelessness, and even avoiding the school-to-prison pipeline.

A JJAEP is generally required to offer English language arts, mathematics, science, social science, and self-discipline (Texas Education Code, 2018). These programs operate under normal 8–4 school-type hours. The participants attend them as if they are attending regular school. Academically, the general mission of JJAEPs is to have the student perform at the appropriate grade level (Texas Education Code, 2018).

Mandatory referrals to JJAEPs are generally reserved for violent or dangerous offenses such as unlawfully carrying a weapon on school grounds. These weapons can be anything from a firearm, knife, explosive device, chemical weapon, brass knuckles, or even parts of weapons, such as ammunition or silencers. In addition to those with weapons charges, these programs are mandatory for violent or aggressive youth who may have been arrested for traditional violent crimes, such as murder, attempted murder, aggravated kidnapping, aggravated sexual assault, arson, manslaughter, or felony drug charges. In addition to these mandatory referrals, there are a multitude of discretionary referrals, such as terroristic threats, possession of marijuana, assault on a student, assault on a teacher/employee, and false alarm offenses.

The independent school districts can operate JJAEPs, but they can also be operated in the private sector for profit. Unfortunately, many private-run organizations do not have to meet the same required guidelines as they are independent of the school districts. As a result, they may be merely "sub-standard disciplinary alternative schools" and often take on detention-like environments by requiring students to undergo repeated searches upon entry, keeping police officers present, and restricting the juveniles' movements (Weissman et al., 2008).

State Commitment Centers

Out of the approximately 60,000 juveniles who are incarcerated across the nation, approximately 36,000 are *committed* to state commitment centers (The Council of State Governments Justice Center, 2015). In the juvenile justice system, juveniles are *committed* and not *sentenced*, as in the adult system. State commitment centers or *institutions* (the term used in the juvenile justice system that means *prisons*) are the last stop for juveniles who have been involved in the juvenile justice system before entering into the adult system. Juveniles who have exhausted all other remedies of rehabilitation in the juvenile system or have committed particularly heinous crimes that are adjudicated will be committed to a state commitment center. Juveniles who are committed by their states can have a range of sentences, but the national average is approximately 3 to 12 months (The Council of State Governments Justice Center, 2015). However, sentences are routinely indeterminate sentences, and as a result of disciplinary infractions, a juvenile may extend the time spent at a commitment center.

State commitment centers will have a larger variety of course offerings than other education-related sanctions. As a result of state institutions being the last stop in the juvenile justice system, many states offer a multitude of trade skill options (auto mechanic, carpentry, electricity, fiber optics, cosmetology, etc.) for the juveniles in custody, along with the traditional academic course offerings. State commitment centers may also provide access to college curriculums (through traditional and nontraditional methods), as these juveniles may have already ascertained their high school diplomas. Online courses are available for students who may be interested in ascertaining training or completing college degrees.

As with all the other education-related sanctions, the juveniles at state commitment centers also have a myriad of issues that need to be circumvented to be successful. One of the main issues at a state commitment center is the difficulty of retaining quality instructors (Berardi, 2017). Despite the fact that state institutions are relatively safe for educators, they can produce high levels of stress for those who may not be accustomed to secure environments.

Behavioral issues can also be a major issue that may need to be addressed at a commitment center. A juvenile may have his or her own behavior issues and attitudes, such as anger management, to address, but he or she will also have to deal with the behaviors and attitudes of the other juveniles who are also in custody. As state institutions are, in fact, prisons for juveniles, they will have the same negative components of an adult prison facility.

Juveniles who are confined in state commitment centers will generally have had multiple opportunities to address their behavioral issues at earlier stages in the juvenile justice system but for whatever reason have failed in deterring themselves from law-violating behavior.

SUMMARY

Juvenile court judges have a range of options before and after adjudicating juveniles. Judges will examine various factors when determining the appropriate disposition of juveniles, including their educational status, as juveniles are, by law, required to attend some type of educational program. However, a judge may have to decide what educational avenues are in the best interest of the juvenile. A judge may require a juvenile to stay in school, complete a GED, or attend an educational program at a detention or residential facility, JJAEP, or state institution.

Despite the multitude of programs that are offered to juveniles who are incarcerated, there are still some educational issues that need to get addressed. Various states do not provide adequate programming or standardized curricula for their students, and there are severe overcrowding issues in their facilities (Twomey, 2008). Each of these issues can severely hamper the educational process and the overall commitment to juveniles' success.

In addition, trying to keep juveniles in school after their release from incarceration may be one of the greater challenges facing juvenile justice agencies. Post-release numbers indicate that out of the estimated 100,000 juveniles who are released from a yearlong incarceration, nearly half of them do not return to school (Mears & Travis, 2004), and of those who do return to school, 16% drop out within the first 5 months (Foley, 2001).

Aftercare supervision is another area of concern for those agencies that are fighting to keep recidivism rates low. Aftercare supervision for juveniles following their release to aid in bridging the gap from the justice system to reintegration into the traditional school system is imperative, as it is generally understood that increased educational achievement will have lasting effects on reducing future criminal behavior (Herz et al., 2012). According to the Guiding Principles for Providing High-Quality Education in Juvenile Justice Secure Care Settings, it is recommended that a reentry plan be initiated immediately upon entry into a secure facility (U.S. Departments of Education and Justice, 2014). Unfortunately, that is rarely happening beyond routine reentry plans that are generalized to all juveniles as a whole and not specialized to meet the specific treatment problems of individual juveniles, such as the continuation of treatment for substance abuse or mental health (Juvenile Justice Information Exchange, 2018).

These are just some of the issues that juvenile justice agencies are addressing to ensure that youth are getting the care and support they need to succeed in school while incarcerated and once released. As new technologies are developed, there will be other opportunities for juveniles to ascertain their education while incarcerated. Technological advancements such as online educational programs need only to ensure that safety- and security-related issues are not hampered at the implementing institution.

DISCUSSION QUESTIONS

1. Why do you think agencies try to avoid detaining youth during the referral process?
2. Keeping the safety of juveniles and staff in mind, what trade school options (mechanics, electrical, computer technology programs, etc.) should be made available to juveniles once they have been committed to a state school?
3. How has education contributed to the decrease in juvenile crime?

REFERENCES

Andrei T., Teodorescu, D., & Oancea, B. (2012). Quantitative methods used to identify the causes of school dropout in EU countries. *Procedia - Social Behavioral Sciences, 31*, 188–192. https://doi.org/10.1016/j.sbspro.2001.12.039.

Austin, J., Johnson, K, & Weitzer, R. (2005). Alternative to secure detention and confinement of juvenile offenders. Office of Juvenile Justice and Delinquency Prevention Bulletin, September 2005, *(5), 1.*

Berardi, F. (2017). For an increasing number of youth in juvenile detention, learning is possible. *Slate.* Retrieved from http://www.slate.com/articles/life/schooled/2017/12/for_an_ increasing _ number _of_ youth_ in_juvenile_detention_learning_is_possible.html

Cortez, A. (1999). Alternative education programs in Texas: More questions than answers. IDRA Newsletter. November–December, 1999. Retrieved from https://www.idra.org/ resouce-center/alternative-education-programs-in-texas/

Foley, R.M. (2001). Academic characteristics of incarcerated youth and correctional educational programs: A literature review. *Journal of Emotional and Behavioral Disorders, 9(4),* 248–259. doi: 10.1177/10632660100900405.

Herrenkohl, T. L., Hawkins, J. D., Chung, I., Hill, K. G., & Battin-Pearson, S. (2001). School and community risk factors and interventions. In R. Loeber & D.P. Farrington (Eds.), *Child delinquents: Development, intervention, and service needs* (pp. 211–246). Thousand Oaks, CA: Sage Publications.

Herz, D., Lee, P., Lutz, L., Stewart, M., Tuell, J., Wiig, J., (2012). *Addressing the needs of multi-system youth: strengthening the connection between child welfare and juvenile justice.* Washington, DC: Center for Juvenile Justice Reform at Georgetown University, Robert F. Kennedy Children's Action Corps.

In re Gault, 387 U.S. 1 (1967).

Juvenile Justice Information Exchange. (2018). Re-entry. Retrieved from https://jjie.org/hub/ reentry/

Kim S. A. (2012). Individual, social factors, and experience after school dropout: Difference between delinquent and non-delinquent dropout youth. *Journal of the Korea Contents Association, 12,* 216–226

Leone, P., & Weinberg, L. (2010). *Addressing the unmet educational needs of children and youth in the juvenile justice and child welfare systems.* Washington, DC: The Center for Juvenile Justice Reform.

McCluskey, M. (2017). The presence of justice: What if this were your kid? *The Atlantic.* Retrieved from https://www.theatlantic.com/politics/archive/2017/12/juvenile-solitary-confinement/548933/

McKeiver v. Pennsylvania, 403 U.S. 528 (1971).

Mears, D. P., & Travis, J. (2004). Youth development and re-entry. *Youth Violence and Juvenile Justice, 2(1),* 3–20.

Moffitt, T. E., Lynam, D. R., & Silva, P.A. (1994). Neuropsychological test predicting persistent male delinquency. *Criminology, 32(2),* 277–300.

National Research Council (2013). *Reforming juvenile justice: A developmental approach.* Washington, DC: The National Academies Press. https: doi.org/10.17226/14685

Seguin, J. R., Pihl, R. O., Harden, P. W., Tremblay, R. E., & Boulerice, B. (1995). Cognitive and neuropsychological characteristics of physically aggressive boys. *Journal of Abnormal Psychology, 104(3),* 614–624. doi: 10.1037/0021-843X.104.4.614

Snyder, H. N., & Sickmund, M. (2006). *Juvenile offenders and victims: 2006 national report.* Washington, DC: U.S. Department of Justice, Office of Justice Programs, Office of Juvenile Justice and Delinquency Prevention.

Texas Education Code (2018). Juvenile Justice Alternative Education Program Section 37.011. Retrieved from http://texas.public.law/statues/tex._educ._code_section_37.011

Texas Lawyers Association (2018). The Texas juvenile justice system: What you need to know. Retrieved from https://www.texasbar.com/AM/Template.cfm?Section=Free_Legal_Information2&Template=/CM/ContentDisplay.cfm&ContentID=26237.

The Council of State Governments Justice Center. (2015). *Locked out: Improving education and vocational outcomes for incarcerated youth.* New York, NY: Author.

Twomey, K. (2008). The right to education in juvenile detention under state constitutions. Virginia Law Review, 94(3), 765–811.

U.S. Departments of Education and Justice. (2014). Guiding Principles for Providing High-Quality Education in Juvenile Justice Secure Care Settings. Washington, DC: Author.

Weissman, M., Cregor, M., Gainsborough, J., Kief, N., Leone, P., & Sullivan, E. (2008). The right to education in the juvenile and criminal justice systems in the United States. Dignity in Schools Campaign (DSC). Report submitted to U.N. Special Rapporteur on the Right to Education. Retrieved from https://www.aclu.org/other/right-education-juvenile-and-criminal-justice-systems-united-states

CHAPTER SEVEN

Juvenile Rights in Educational Settings

Georgen Guerrero and Katalin Parti

READING OBJECTIVES

- Understand the development and the foundation of juvenile court proceedings, with special regard to First and Fourth Amendment rights.
- Identify the due process rights juveniles are entitled to. Identify the situations that determine when schools have the right to curtail students' rights.
- Define the intent of the juvenile justice system and how it is aimed at addressing the needs of children rather than adjudicating and punishing criminal behavior.
- Explain the importance of the reorganization of the juvenile justice system.
- Explain the necessity of U.S. Supreme Court landmark decisions in off-campus (online) student speech cases.
- Summarize the efforts of courts regulating students' constitutional rights.

OVERVIEW

This chapter will address the landmark decisions of the U.S. Supreme Court (USSC) on students' rights for a juvenile court proceeding, freedom of speech, and their rights against search and seizure. These decisions of the USSC, dating back to the second half of the 20th century, are still used as guidelines for students' rights in schools. Jurisprudence reaches out to these decisions, even in juvenile justice cases that have happened across the street from a school campus, online, or even off-campus. The chapter highlights the ambiguities of these landmark decisions, suggesting that more up-to-date legislation would be required to maintain cases related to the increasingly popular online sites of communication. The chapter concludes that although juveniles' rights in criminal procedures became recognized, schools remain empowered to restrict students' citizen rights in avoidance of a foreseeable risk of substantial disruption within the school.

LANDMARK USSC CASES

The juvenile justice system was built in 1899 under the concept of parens patriae: the right of the government to act in the "best interest of the child," acting as the parent of the child (Lab, 2013). Under *parens patriae,* juveniles were not seen as needing the same due process constitutional protections as adults. The court, acting as the parent, would protect the juvenile from the abuses and misfortunes of the criminal justice system and, therefore, juveniles were not in need of due process protections. However, during the 1960s, the USSC started to examine some of the basic premises of the juvenile justice system, specifically that it did not have due process protections under *parens patriae.* The 1960s produced several landmark cases that revolutionized the juvenile justice system.

Kent v. United States (1966)

The first of these landmark cases, *Kent v. United States* (1966), examined the waiving of a juvenile from a juvenile court to an adult court. Morris A. Kent Jr., a 16-year-old male, was taken into custody and interrogated as part of a police investigation involving charges of housebreaking, robbery, and rape. During the interrogation, Kent admitted to some guilt. The juvenile court waived its jurisdiction to the U.S. district court for the District of Columbia, resulting in Kent being indicted in adult court. The petitioner's counsel moved to dismiss the indictment, arguing that the waiver was invalid. Counsel argued that the District of Columbia Juvenile Court did not complete a "full investigation" as statutorily required by the Juvenile Court Act (*Kent v. United States*, 1966). The district court overruled the motion, and Kent was tried as an adult. Kent was found guilty in the jury trial on six counts of housebreaking and robbery but was acquitted on all counts of rape by reason of insanity. He was sentenced to serve 30–90 years in prison (*Kent v. United States*, 1966). The U.S. court of appeals for the District of Columbia Circuit affirmed the ruling, but it noted that no reason was provided for the waiver by the juvenile court.

In deciding to hear the case, the USSC examined if the juvenile waiver to adult court was valid. The Court determined that a juvenile waiver to adult court was a "critical stage" in juvenile court proceedings (*Kent v. United States*, 1966). The USSC ruled that prior to waiving a juvenile to the adult system, the prosecution needed to put specific findings in writing, outlining why a juvenile should be transferred over to a criminal court. The Court ruled that juveniles had the right to a hearing on the matter, to be represented by counsel at that hearing, to have access to the records considered by the juvenile court, and to receive a statement of reasons for the waiver.

In Re Gault (1967)

In re Gault (1967) was a landmark Supreme Court case that established that juveniles facing the possibility of incarceration were entitled to the same due process rights as adults. The issue raised in In re Gault was "are juveniles entitled to due process protections during the adjudication phase of delinquency proceedings?" In an 8–1 decision, the Court ruled in favor of Gault, stating that his Sixth Amendment rights had been violated; specifically, the right to an attorney, the right of notification of charges against him, the right against self-incrimination, and the right to confront his accusers (*In re Gault*, 1967).

The *In re Gault* case concerned a 15-year-old male named Gerald Francis Gault who was on probation. He was taken into custody at 10:00 a.m. for allegedly making obscene phone calls to one of his neighbors, Ora Cook, with one of his friends, Ronald Lewis. Both of Gault's parents were at work and not aware that he had been taken into custody (*In re Gault*, 1967). The arresting officer made no attempt to contact Gault's parents nor did he leave any notice for them.

At approximately 6:00 p.m., Gault's mother returned home, and she was unable to locate Gault. She had Gault's older brother go and look for him at Ronald's home. The Lewis family advised him that Gault had been taken into custody earlier in the day. Gault's mother went to the Children's Detention Home and was informed of the reason he was taken into custody and that he would have a hearing the next day (*In re Gault*, 1967).

A hearing was held in the judge's chambers where a petition was filed that made general allegations of delinquency. No specific facts were offered in the petition; it merely stated that the "minor is under the age of eighteen years and is in need of the protection of this Honorable Court" (*In re Gault*, 1967). During the proceedings, no one was sworn in, no attorney was present, the complainant was not present, and no records of the proceeding were made. Gault stated that he did not make any of the lewd comments but did admit to dialing the phone number (*In re Gault*, 1967). He stated that he had overheard what Ronald was saying and then told him to get out. The judge stated that he would consider the matter (*In re Gault*, 1967). Gault was returned to the Children's Detention Home and released 2 days later (*In re Gault*, 1967).

Six days later, a delinquency hearing was held without any assistance of counsel, complaining witnesses, sworn testimony, or transcript of the hearing (*In re Gault*, 1967). Gault's probation officer was present and submitted a referral report to the court listing the charge as lewd phone calls (*In re Gault*, 1967). The report was not presented to Gault or his parents. The presiding judge committed Gault to the State Industrial School until the age of 21 (*In re Gault*, 1967). Gault had received a 6-year sentence for a minor crime that an adult would have received a $5–$50 fine or 2 months in jail for (*In re Gault*, 1967).

The issue for the USSC in the *In re Gault* case was "should juveniles have the same due process rights during the adjudication stage of a delinquency proceeding as adults have in criminal proceedings?" The Court found that they do have due process rights and that they are entitled to

1. the right to reasonable notice of charges;
2. the right to counsel;
3. the right to confront and cross-examine; and
4. the right against self-incrimination, including the right to remain silent.

The importance of the *In re Gault* case goes beyond simply allowing juveniles the right to due process. The *In re Gault* case was a defining moment in the reorganization of the juvenile justice system. The juvenile justice system was no longer an informal juvenile court process operating under the guise of *parens patriae* but more of a formalized adversarial court.

In Re Winship (1970)

In 1970, the *In re Winship* case elevated the standard of proof to *proof beyond a reasonable doubt* in the juvenile system whenever there was the possibility of depriving a juvenile of his or her liberty. The original intent of the juvenile justice system was to rehabilitate the children in its care. It was theoretically established under the guise of addressing the needs of children rather than adjudicating and punishing criminal behavior.

The state would act accordingly through the concept of *parens patriae* rather than through an adversarial system with a prosecuting attorney and judge. As a result of this original intent, the processing of a juvenile through the justice system was considered civil and not criminal; therefore, the court maintained the lower standard of proof of *preponderance of the evidence*. With a juvenile's freedom now being decided in the juvenile system, the USSC had to consider if juveniles had the same due process rights as adults when being deprived of their freedom by enhancing the level of proof required in all future juvenile hearings.

In the case of *In re Winship* (1970), Samuel Winship, a 12-year-old New York juvenile male, was charged with taking $112 from a woman's purse. If this crime had been committed by an adult, the individual would have been charged with larceny (*In re Winship*, 1970). He was adjudicated as a delinquent based on the preponderance of the evidence standard. He was committed to a training school for 18 months, with a possible extension until he was 18 years old for a total possible sentence of 6 years.

The issue raised in the *In re Winship* case was whether the preponderance of the evidence standard that was used instead of proof beyond a reasonable doubt as required in adult criminal proceedings violated the Constitution's due process clause of the Fourteenth Amendment. The State of New York argued that matters resolved through the juvenile justice system were civil and not criminal; therefore, it did not require proof beyond a reasonable doubt (*In re Winship*, 1970).

The Supreme Court disagreed with the trial court and the court of appeals and ruled in favor of the juvenile, stating that when a juvenile is faced with a proceeding in which incarceration might result, the standard of proof beyond a reasonable doubt should be applied (*In re Winship*, 1970). The Court clarified that when a juvenile is on trial for delinquent behavior and the possibility of incarceration exists, the beyond a reasonable doubt standard is constitutionally required (*In re Winship*, 1970).

McKeiver v. Pennsylvania (1971)

Despite allowing juveniles to claim several Constitutional rights, the USSC did not completely overhaul the entire juvenile justice system during the due process revolution of the 1960s. In *McKeiver v. Pennsylvania*, the USSC ruled against Joseph McKeiver and Edward Terry, who were charged with acts of robbery, theft, assault, and escape, when it ruled that juveniles do not have a Constitutional right to trial by jury in accordance to the Sixth or Fourteenth Amendments (*McKeiver v. Pennsylvania*, 1971). At trial, the juveniles' request for a trial by jury was denied (*McKeiver v. Pennsylvania*, 1971). In ruling against the juveniles, the USSC upheld the trial court's decision, an affirmation from a Superior Court, and another affirmation by the Supreme Court of Pennsylvania, all of whom had stated that juveniles do not have a Constitutional right to a trial by jury (*McKeiver v. Pennsylvania*, 1971).

FOURTH AMENDMENT RIGHT AGAINST UNREASONABLE SEARCH AND SEIZURE

The Fourth Amendment protects people from unreasonable searches and seizures. It prohibits the government from illegally taking property, papers, or people without a valid warrant based on *probable cause*. As school safety has become a high priority for educational administrators, the rights of juveniles need to be examined. Finding a balance between school safety and individual student rights is paramount.

New Jersey v. T.L.O. (1985)

In 1985, the right to search an individual under the *reasonable suspicion* standard was at the heart of *New Jersey v. T.L.O.* (1985). T.L.O. was a 14-year-old freshman who was witnessed by a teacher smoking a cigarette with another student in the school restroom in violation of the rules (*New Jersey v. T.L.O.*, 1985). The two students were taken to the principal's office and questioned by the assistant vice principal, and T.L.O. denied smoking the cigarettes in question (*New Jersey v. T.L.O.*, 1985). The assistant vice principal demanded to see T.L.O.'s purse and searched it after she denied the allegations. During the search, he found a pack of cigarettes, cigarette rolling paper, a pipe, a small plastic bag that contained a grass-like substance, a wad of money, an index card with the names of several students who owed her money, and two letters that indicated that she was selling marijuana at school (*New Jersey v. T.L.O.*, 1985).

The assistant vice principal contacted the police and provided them with the items that were removed from T.L.O.'s purse. The police contacted T.L.O.'s mother, and the mother brought her to the police station where she confessed to selling marijuana. Using the items found in T.L.O.'s purse and the confession that T.L.O. had provided to the police, delinquency charges were filed against her.

Prior to trial, the defendant's attorney submitted a motion to suppress the evidence from the search and suppress the confession that was provided by T.L.O., arguing that her Fourth Amendment right against unreasonable searches and seizures was violated (*New Jersey v. T.L.O.*, 1985). The trial court denied the motion. The Juvenile and Domestic Relations Court of New Jersey adjudicated her as a delinquent and placed her on probation for a year. Her attorney appealed to the Superior Court of New Jersey, Appellate Division, but the Superior Court affirmed the decision. However, the New Jersey Supreme Court disagreed with the two lower courts and reversed the decision, ruling that the **exclusionary rule** applies to searches and seizures that are conducted by administrative officials in public schools (*New Jersey v. T.L.O.*, 1985).

The USSC granted certiorari to hear New Jersey v. T.L.O in 1984 to examine if the exclusionary rule applies to searches conducted by school officials in public school. On January 15, 1985, the USSC ruled in *New Jersey v. T.L.O.* (1985) with a 6–3 decision that the school's search of T.L.O.'s purse was constitutional, ruling that administrators can search a student's personal possessions if they have reasonable suspicion that a violation of a campus rule has taken place or that criminal behavior is occurring (*New Jersey v. T.L.O.*, 1985). The USSC ruled that even though students have "legitimate expectations of privacy," schools had a responsibility to maintain "an environment in which learning can take place" (*New Jersey v. T.L.O.*, 1985). As a result of the teacher's report that she observed T.L.O. smoking in a bathroom, which prompted the initial search of her purse, the search was justified and the subsequent discovery of the items in T.L.O.'s purse was acceptable. The ruling was a huge victory for school administrators in every school, in every state, all across the country. It allows school administrators to conduct warrantless searches of students' possessions without having to meet the probable cause standard that is required by law enforcement officials.

Vernonia School District 47J v. Acton (1995)

The USSC examined a more personal search and seizure issue in *Vernonia School District 47J v. Acton* (1995; hereinafter *Vernonia School District v. Acton*, 1995). The USSC in a 6–3 decision ruled against students by allowing school administrators to conduct random drug testing of school athletes. In 1995, James Acton, a 12-year-old seventh grader, wanted to try out for the football team at Washington Grade School in Vernonia, Oregon (*Vernonia School District v. Acton*, 1995). School rules required all student athletes to submit to an initial drug test before the beginning of the football season and then participate in random drug testing throughout the school year. Acton's parents objected to the drug test on the premise that there was no history of any prior alcohol or drug use. James was suspended from the football team and Acton's parents sued the school district on the basis that a drug test without any suspicion of drug or alcohol use was unwarranted and a violation of the Fourth Amendment right against unreasonable searches and seizures (*Vernonia School District v. Acton*, 1995).

In wanting to address the issues of school safety, specifically drug use, among student athletes, the USSC ruled that a minimal invasion of privacy did not violate the Fourth Amendment's ban on unreasonable searches and seizures. The Supreme Court vocalized that student athletes should generally expect less privacy than students who were not athletes. As student athletes, they are generally expected to undergo physical examinations, dress and shower in locker rooms, and even maintain acceptable grade point averages (*Vernonia School District v. Acton*, 1995). As a result, student athletes do give up certain expectations of privacy when engaging in athletic competition when representing local school districts. Therefore, a requirement by school officials to have student athletes undergo drug testing was not considered unconstitutional.

Board of Education of Independent School District No. 92 of Pottawatomie City v. Earls (2002)

A few years later in *Board of Education of Independent School District No. 92 of Pottawatomie City v. Earls* (2002; hereinafter *Education v. Earls*, 2002), the Supreme Court broadened the scope of schools' drug testing policies when it examined a similar drug testing policy in Oklahoma. In a 5–4 decision, the Supreme Court ruled that schools may require mandatory drug testing for all students who participate in extracurricular activities. In this particular case, Tecumseh, Oklahoma, School District of Pottawatomie County required all middle and high school students to undergo urinalysis testing to participate in any extracurricular activity (*Education v. Earls*, 2002). The legal challenge to this practice was brought on by two of the students, along with their parents at Tecumseh High School. The students and their parents argued that this was a violation of their Fourth Amendment right against unreasonable searches and seizures (*Education v. Earls*, 2002). The district court granted summary judgment in favor of the school district; however, the court of appeals reversed the district court decision. The court of appeals argued that in imposing a suspicionless drug testing policy, the school should be able to demonstrate that there was a need for such a policy among a substantial number of those who were tested (*Education v. Earls*, 2002). The implementation of this mandatory drug testing policy would allow the school to actually redress the drug problem within that population of students.

However, the Supreme Court disagreed with the appellate court and ruled against the students, arguing that there was a diminished expectation of privacy for anyone who was participating in extracurricular activities. The policy furthered an important interest of the school in preventing drug use among students and noted that the use of urinalysis was minimally intrusive on the students' limited expectation of privacy (*Education v. Earls*, 2002). *Education v. Earls* (2002) strengthened mandatory drug testing programs in schools and expanded the Court's ruling in *Vernonia School District v. Acton* (1995).

FIRST AMENDMENT RIGHT TO FREEDOM OF SPEECH

As adults continue to question and speak out against traditional repressive regimes, such as tyranny, oppression, and bureaucracy, students too have taken up many similar stances against the American educational system. As a result of the numerous rules and regulations that are present in educational systems in America, they offer students great opportunities to question the legality of some of these rules and regulations that are generally set upon them by their independent school districts.

The right of the people to practice a religion of their choice freely, to speak freely, to peaceably assemble, to petition the government for a redress of grievances and the right to a free press can all be found in the Bill of Rights under the First Amendment. The *Tinker v. Des Moines Independent Community School District* (1969) is a landmark case that is routinely cited today by the USSC. In First Amendment cases involving the freedom of speech, it is well regarded as the most influential case in American school history, protecting the rights of students under the First Amendment. Tinker allowed the Court to examine the rights of students on school grounds. This case is well known for Justice Fortas's statement: "It can hardly be argued that either students or teachers shed their constitutional rights to free speech at the schoolhouse gate" (*Tinker v. Des Moines Independent Community School District*, 1969). The Supreme Court examined two additional cases that involved freedom of speech: *Bethel School District No. 403 v. Fraser* and *Hazelwood School District v. Kuhlmeier*. In both of these cases, the Court rejected students' rights and sided with the schools.

Tinker v. Des Moines Independent Community School District (1969)

A 15-year-old student from Des Moines, Iowa, John Tinker, along with his 13-year-old sister Mary Beth Tinker, 11-year-old sister Hope Tinker, and 8-year-old brother Paul Tinker assembled in the home of 16-year-old Chris Eckhardt and strategized to wear black bands around their arms to their respective schools in support of Robert Kennedy's Christmas Truce and protest of the Vietnam War, in December of 1965 (*Tinker v. Des Moines Independent Community School District*, 1969). Their original intent was to wear the black bands on their arms throughout the holiday season from December 16 all the way to January 1.

On December 14, the Des Moines, Iowa, school district, having heard of the students' intentions to wear the armbands, created a policy that would restrict the students from wearing them (*Tinker v. Des Moines Independent Community School District*, 1969). The school policy would be simple in that any students observed wearing one of the armbands would simply be asked to remove it or endure a school suspension until they complied with the school policy (*Tinker v. Des Moines Independent Community School District*, 1969).

The first day that the students arrived on-campus wearing the armbands, December 16, both Christopher Eckhardt and Mary Beth Tinker were suspended from their respective schools, while John Tinker was suspended from his school on the following day. All three of the students were suspended from their respective schools until January 1, the day that they had initially planned to conclude their protest. The two younger Tinker students, Hope (11 years old) and Paul (8 years old), were not suspended at all (*Tinker v. Des Moines Independent Community School District*, 1969). In fact, their teachers used the opportunity as a chance to teach and discuss the situation with their students.

The families, with the support of the American Civil Liberties Union, filed a suit with the U.S. district court, arguing that the suspension violated their constitutional right of free speech. The U.S. district court upheld the decision of the Des Moines, Iowa, school board to suspend the students. The U.S. court of appeals upheld the decision through a tie vote, resulting in a direct appeal to the USSC.

The USSC addressed two main issues in *Tinker v. Des Moines Independent Community School District* (1969). The first concern for the Court was if First Amendment rights were owned by schoolchildren, while at school versus only belonging to adults in a free society. Do students shed their First Amendment rights when they enter school grounds (i.e., "at the schoolhouse gate")? (*Tinker v. Des Moines Independent Community School District*, 1969). The Supreme Court ruled in favor of the students with a 7–2 vote, stating that neither students nor teachers shed their First Amendment rights just because they enter onto school grounds.

The second issue in question was if wearing the black armband as a symbolic protest was, in fact, a form of "free speech" protected by the First Amendment (*Tinker v. Des Moines Independent Community School District*, 1969). The school district had taken the position that schools were a place for education and not a place for active protest. However, the USSC ruled principally in the students' favor, stating that the wearing of the armband was, in fact, a form of free speech that is protected by the First Amendment. The Supreme Court stated that the students did not produce any disorder in the classroom or hamper the learning environment but merely encouraged discussion outside of the classrooms (*Tinker v. Des Moines Independent Community School District*, 1969). However, the Supreme Court did note that schools had a responsibility to maintain safety and security. Therefore, the Court did not offer students an unlimited right to self-expression through the First Amendment's right to freedom of speech. In reality, the Supreme Court limited the students' free speech, noting that it would be permissible as long as it did not inhibit or interfere with student learning or cause any significant disruption at school. In deciding this case, the Supreme Court established the "disruption test" where they answered the question, did the speech or expression of the student "materially and substantially interfere with the requirements of appropriate discipline in the operation of the school" (*Tinker v. Des Moines Independent Community School District*, 1969).

Since its inception in the Tinker case, the "disruption test" has been repeatedly cited by lower courts and the USSC to help preserve order in schools (*Tinker v. Des Moines Independent Community School District*, 1969). In 1986, Tinker was reexamined by the Supreme Court when Matthew Fraser, a student at the Bethel School District, was suspended and declared ineligible as a graduation speaker after delivering a school campaign speech containing sexual innuendos.

Bethel School District No. 403 v. Fraser (1986)

In April of 1983, Matthew Fraser, a 17-year-old student at Bethel High School in Washington, gave a nomination speech in support of one of his classmates with numerous sexual innuendos and references, but it did not have any obscene language (*Bethel School District #403 v. Fraser*, 1986). He was warned not to give the speech by two different administrators and that if he did, serious consequences could result. When Fraser delivered the speech, the audience reacted in a variety of ways; some appeared to be embarrassed; others yelled and made obscene gestures (*Bethel School District #403 v. Fraser*, 1986). As a result of the highly charged nomination speech, Fraser was suspended for three days and had his name removed from a list of three potential graduation speakers (*Bethel School District #403 v. Fraser*, 1986). Despite being removed as a potential speaker, Fraser had finished second overall among the top-three finishers via write-in votes by the school's student body (*Bethel School District #403 v. Fraser*, 1986).

Fraser appealed the decision through the school's grievance procedure but was still found to be in violation of school policies against disruptive behavior and the use of vulgar and offensive speech (*Bethel School District #403 v. Fraser*, 1986). Fraser filed a lawsuit against the school claiming that his First Amendment right of free speech was violated, and when the school removed his name from a list of potential graduation speakers, they violated the due process clause of the Fourteenth Amendment. The U.S. district court ruled in his favor, and the school appealed to the Ninth Circuit Court of Appeals. The Ninth Circuit Court upheld the ruling arguing that Fraser's speech was no different than the student speech in *Tinker v. Des Moines Independent Community School District*. The school requested certiorari to the Supreme Court, and it was accepted.

In a landmark decision, the USSC voted 7–2 against Fraser when it held that it was constitutional for a school "to prohibit the use of vulgar and offensive terms in public discourse" (*Bethel School District #403 v. Fraser*, 1986). The school did not violate Fraser's constitutional right of free speech nor did it infringe on the child's due process rights. The Court argued that the armbands in *Tinker v. Des Moines* were not associated with the school and were political in nature, while Fraser's school speech was directly related to the school and was not political in nature; therefore, the school did have a vested interest in prohibiting certain styles of expression that were sexually vulgar. As a result, *Bethel School District No. 403 v. Fraser* limited students' First Amendment right of free speech on school grounds.

Hazelwood School District v. Kuhlmeier (1988)

In another landmark case, *Hazelwood School District v. Kuhlmeier* (1998), the USSC ruled against students with a 5–3 vote, allowing public schools to censor school newspapers. The Court reasoned that school newspapers are not public forums where students are able to claim their First Amendment right to freedom of speech (*Hazelwood School District v. Kuhlmeier*, 1998).

In 1983, the principal at Hazelwood East High School in St. Louis County, Missouri, Robert Eugene Reynolds, removed two articles in the school newspaper, The Spectrum, prior to publication. The articles were written by students in a Journalism II course (*Hazelwood School District v. Kuhlmeier*, 1998). The first article was on the effect of divorce on students, which made a reference to a specific student, but that student's name was going to be covered using a pseudonym prior to publication. The principal believed that the family should have been given an opportunity to respond to the story or to object to its publication (*Hazelwood School District v. Kuhlmeier*, 1998).

The second article was on student pregnancies, which provided positive accounts of the experiences of three pregnant students using pseudonyms to protect their identities. The principal believed that the article was inappropriate for younger students as it made references to sexual activity and birth control methods. In response, editor Cathy Kuhlmeier and reporters Leslie Smart and Leann Tippett, with the aid of the American Civil Liberties Union, claimed that their First Amendment rights had been violated and filed suit (*Hazelwood School District v. Kuhlmeier*, 1998).

The Court upheld the prohibition as constitutional. The Court ruled in favor of the public school, stating that the school newspaper was a curriculum-based, school-sponsored learning experience and not an open public forum for students to voice opinions. The ruling allows schools to censor other school-related supervised learning activities, such as yearbooks, theatrical productions, and graduation speeches.

Morse v. Frederick (2007)

In another Supreme Court case, *Morse v. Frederick* (2007), the Court ruled 5–4 against students by restricting free speech in schools or even across the street when a student appears to be encouraging illegal drug use during a school-supervised event. In this particular case, Joseph Frederick was suspended for displaying a sign across the street from his school during the Olympic torch relay that read "Bong Hits 4 Jesus" (*Morse v. Frederick*, 2007).

On January 24, 2002, the Olympic Torch was to pass by Juneau-Douglas High School on the way to the Winter Olympic Games in Salt Lake City (*Morse v. Frederick*, 2007). The administration at the high school decided to allow the faculty and students to observe the event, and they were excused from their respective classes. The students gathered across the street off-campus on their own accord in what was a nonsponsored school event. Joseph Frederick, an 18-year-old at Juneau-Douglas High School in Alaska who had arrived late to school, joined his friends across the street from the high school (*Morse v. Frederick*, 2007). Waiting for the precise moment when the television camera would be present, the students unrolled a large banner that said, "BONG HITS 4 JESUS" (*Morse v. Frederick*, 2007). Despite the banner not causing a school disruption, the school principal, Deborah Morse, immediately ran across the street and instructed Frederick to take it down, as she was concerned that it could be promoting illegal drug activity. He refused to do so, and she promptly seized the sign. Morse suspended Frederick for 10 days for violating the school's antidrug policy.

After exhausting all internal appeals with the superintendent and the Juneau school board, Frederick filed a civil rights lawsuit claiming that his state and federal rights to free speech were violated (*Morse v. Frederick*, 2007). The U.S. District Court for the District of Alaska dismissed the case on summary judgment. The district court reasoned that *Bethel v. Fraser* and not *Tinker v. Des Moines* should govern Frederick's school speech and ruled in favor of the school district, stating that they had not infringed on his First Amendment rights because the banner was in clear violation of the school antidrug policy (*Morse v. Frederick*, 2007).

Frederick appealed to the Ninth Circuit, and the panel of judges unanimously reversed the district court's decision. The Ninth Circuit Court ruled that it was actually *Tinker v. Des Moines* that should be the controlling analysis and not *Bethel v. Fraser* or *Hazelwood v. Kuhlmeier* (*Morse v. Frederick*, 2007). The appeals court reasoned that Bethel v. Fraser was focused on sexual innuendos that could be restricted on school grounds, while *Hazelwood v. Kuhlmeier* involved a supervised learning activity (*Morse v. Frederick*, 2007). Frederick's banner was neither sexual in nature nor was it under the guise of a supervised learning activity. However, as a result of the ongoing debate for the legalization of marijuana in the state and the federal government, Frederick's banner could be interpreted as political in nature; therefore, the district court's decision was reversed (*Morse v. Frederick*, 2007).

The school petitioned to the Supreme Court, and the Court reversed the Ninth Circuit Court's decision, ruling in favor of the school. In ruling for the school, the Supreme Court examined three key issues. First, it determined that the banner speech in this case did fall under the school speech jurisprudence (*Morse v. Frederick*, 2007).

The Court noted that even though the children were across the street away from the school, they were still in the presence of school administrators; one could not reasonably expect a superintendent to be in the presence of students and not act in his or her official capacity. Second, the Court reasoned that the principal did, in fact, reasonably interpret the sign as advocating for the use of illegal drugs (*Morse v. Frederick*, 2007). Third, the Court concluded that the school speech jurisprudence does apply in trying to keep a school safe and, therefore, the school could restrict Frederick's speech because it promoted drug use (*Morse v. Frederick*, 2007).

THE USSC DECISIONS' APPLICABILITY TO OFF-CAMPUS SPEECH CASES

Whether students' free speech can be limited by schools depending on the location where the speech is conducted is an ongoing debate (Ho, 2012; Pongó, 2015). Tinker's "schoolhouse gate" formula has a significant importance in electronic speech cases, as online speech can happen anywhere, even outside of school, yet can well have an effect at school. According to the Tinker standards, the school is entitled to restrict freedom of speech either when "it reasonably forecasts a substantial disruption because of the expression, or it collides with the rights of others" (McCarthy, 2014, p. 813). Online speech conveying hatred or cyberbullying does not necessarily disrupt the school climate, but it surely collides with the rights of the person targeted.

Wisniewski v. Board of Education of Weedsport Central School District (2007)
Aaron Wisniewski, an eighth grader, was using an instant messenger (IM) program at his parents' computer at home (i.e., off-campus). Aaron, when using the IM program, displayed an icon for his self-identification, which was a small drawing of a pistol firing a bullet at a person's head, above which were small dots representing blood. Beneath this icon, he wrote, "Kill Mr. VanderMolen," referring to his English teacher. He displayed it to 15 members of the IM group for 3 weeks. A student showed the drawing to Mr. VanderMolen, who forwarded it to the school principals. Aaron admitted the act, and he was suspended for 5 days. Furthermore, he was subjected to an interview by a police investigator and a psychologist. Both the investigator and the psychologist declared that he had no violent intent and posed no threat to the school employees or the school environment. However, the superintendent held that the icon was threatening and disrupted the school environment. Therefore, Aaron was charged for violation of school rules and suspended for a semester. A year later, his parents filed a suit against the superintendent and the school board for violating Aaron's freedom of speech.

The district court determined that the icon was "reasonably to be understood as a 'true threat,'" therefore, it could not be protected by the First Amendment. On appeal, the Second Circuit applied Tinker's reasonably foreseeable disruption test and claimed that Aaron's online off-campus activity was not protected by freedom of speech. However, the Court came to its decision not by transforming Aaron's speech into an on-campus activity but by applying Tinker to online, off-campus expression. They declared that even "off campus conduct can create a foreseeable risk of substantial disruption within a school" (*Wisniewski v. United States*, 1969, pp. 11–12).

J. C. v. Beverly Hills Unified School District (2009)

J. C. was a high school student who recorded a video about her and her friends' targeting C. C., another student, with profane and vulgar language in a restaurant after school. Later, J. C. uploaded this video to YouTube from her home computer and encouraged five students, including C. C., to watch it. C. C. showed the video to school officials and expressed humiliation and hurt, therefore, she skipped a class. Although YouTube was blocked on school computers, so the students could not watch the video on-campus, J. C. was suspended for 2 days because of her actions. J. C. filed a suit for violation of her First Amendment rights.

The U.S. District Court for the Central District of California first determined the scope of the school's authority to regulate off-campus speech by its students that has an effect on-campus. The Court cited circuit court decisions of off-campus cases that "reached the campus" and thus became on-campus cases through interpretation. The Court, among other cases, cited *Lavine v. Blaine School District* (2001) for applying the USSC student speech tests: (1) vulgar, lewd, obscene, plainly offensive speech governed by Fraser; (2) school-sponsored speech governed by Hazelwood; and (3) other speech that is not covered is governed by Tinker (*J. C. v. Beverly Hills Unified School District*, 2009, p. 13). The speech tests were later supplemented by *Morse v. Frederick* (2007), which governs student on-campus cases regarding illegal drug use. The court held that school administrators would have had an authority to discipline students for off-campus speech if such speech caused a substantial disruption at school. However, the mere fact that students were overheard discussing the video and that the subject of the video was upset by the conversation did not demonstrate a substantial disruption to school activities in the current case.

The foregoing decisions underline the necessity of USSC landmark decisions in cyberbullying cases, which happen online and not necessarily on-campus, to guide school officials and the courts in how to handle such cases, which have significant disruptive effects on the school environment (Pongó, 2016). So far, only Tinker is applicable to students' online speech with an on-campus effect, although happening off-campus. Until specific cyberbullying tests are created by the USSC, it is recommended to determine if the speech (1) is to be considered on or off-campus and if (2) it has a significant disruptive effect on the school environment. If the speech is treated as on-campus, then courts should apply the special USSC on-campus tests (Fraser, Hazelwood, Morse), and if off-campus, then the general Tinker test should be used (Pongó, 2016).

SUMMARY

The 1960s produced several landmark cases that revolutionized the juvenile justice system. These cases lead to the establishment of the due process rights juveniles are entitled to in criminal proceedings. The juvenile justice system is no longer an informal juvenile court process operating under the guise of *parens patriae*, but more of a formalized adversarial court.

Although juveniles' rights became fully recognized in the criminal justice system, schools still remain entitled to limit students' rights to enhance school safety and redress drug problems within schools. The schools' authority covers exclusionary rules to searches and seizures of students (e.g., to conduct warrantless searches without having to meet the probable cause standard and to conduct random drug testing of athletes representing a school district).

There are several USSC decisions interpreting schools' authority to regulate students' speech. However, most of the cases deal with off-campus originated speech, which then has significant effects on-campus but without itself becoming on-campus speech. There is a need for landmark USSC decisions in newly emerging online speech cases.

DISCUSSION QUESTIONS

1. What were the cornerstones in the development of the current juvenile justice system?
2. Along what principles can school administrators practice search and seizure on students?
3. Why do you think it is necessary to curtail students' rights for free speech on-campus?
4. What are the obstacles involved in applying these limitations to off campus speech?
5. Name some current cases from the media in which students' online communication was restricted. Toward what direction do you think schools' rights will develop with the evolution of online communication? What do you think will matter in deciding if online speech is on or off-campus?

REFERENCES

Bethel School District No. 403 v. Fraser, 478 U.S. 675 (1986).

Board of Education of Independent School District No. 92 of Pottawatomie County v. Earls, 536 U.S. 822 (2002).

Hazelwood School District v. Kuhlmeier, 484 U.S. 260 (1988).

Ho, J. (2012). Bullied to death: Cyberbullying and student online speech cases. *Florida Law Review, 64,* 789–816.

In re Gault, 387 U.S. 1 (1967).

In re Winship, 397 U.S. 358 (1970).

J. C. v. Beverly Hills Unified School District, 711 F. Supp. 2d 1094, 1117 (C.D. Cal. 2010) (2009).

Kent v. United States, 383 U.S. 541 (1966).

Lab, S. P., & Williams, M. R. (2016). *Criminal justice: The essentials.* New York, NY: Oxford University Press.

Lavine v. Blaine School District, 257 F. 3d 981, Court of Appeals, 9th Circuit (2001).

Lush, K. (2000). Expanding the rights of children in public schools. *New England Journal on Crime & Civil Confinement, 26,* 95.

McCarthy, M. (2014). Cyberbullying laws and first amendment rulings: Can they be reconciled? *Mississippi Law Journal, 83(4),* 805–837.

McKeiver v. Pennsylvania, 403 U.S. 528 (1971).

Morse v. Frederick, 551 U.S. 393 (2007).

New Jersey v. T.L.O., 469 U.S. 325 (1985).

Pongó, T. (2015). Anglo-Saxon approaches to students' freedom of speech and cyberbullying: Constitutional foundations for a comparative analysis, In S.C. Universul Juridic S.R.L. (Ed.), *Iustum Aequum Salutare. European legal studies and research,* Timisoara (pp. 534–546).

Pongó, T. (2016). Is there a reasonably foreseeable substantial change in US cyberbullying jurisprudence or the ambiguity remains? *Ars Boni, 6(3),* 34–51.

Tinker v. Des Moines Independent Community School District, 393 U.S. 503 (1969).

Vernonia School District 47J v. Acton, 515 U.S. 646 (1995).

Watts v. United States, 394 U.S. 705, 708 (1969).

Wisniewski v. Board of Education of Weedsport Central School District, United States Court of Appeals for the Second Circuit 494 F. 3d 34 (2007).

CHAPTER EIGHT

Peer Mediation

O. Oko Elechi

READING OBJECTIVES

- Introduce the reader to the concept and practice of peer mediation and methods of reducing student-to-student and student-to-teacher conflicts.
- Examine students' negotiation and collaborative problem-solving skills and values.
- Promote caring, social, emotional, responsible, and supportive learning environments.
- Enhance student-to-student and student-to-teacher relationships.
- Inculcate in the students the values of respect, fairness, empathy, nonviolence, trust, tolerance, and inclusive negotiation and mediation skills.

OVERVIEW

The primary goal of schools is the personal and professional development of youth. Schools, especially at the middle and high school levels, are important in the socialization of youth, which is critical for their life chances. Youth at this phase of their lives are going through tough social, mental, and emotional development changes. They are often susceptible to many behavioral influences outside their families, including that of their peers and the media. All these factors contribute to the disciplinary challenges facing the school system. Furthermore, conflict is inevitable in any community. Pretending it does not exist is a disservice to the well-being of the community. Allowing conflict to escalate into verbal or physical violence is disruptive to schools' learning mission. To restore law and order in the school system, school administrators employ several disciplinary measures, including scolding, time-out rooms, suspension, and expulsion. These traditional disciplinary measures require adults to monitor students' behaviors and enforce school rules and policies. Unfortunately, some of these disciplinary practices perpetuate the problem that they are purported to solve. Above all, the learning environment is perverted and, therefore, counterproductive. As such, children fail to learn and peace and order in the school is undermined.

Children learn better and are likely to be more productive when they feel safe and comfortable in their learning environments. The goal of the peer mediation program is to teach students peer mediation skills to enable them to peacefully mediate disputes that may arise among them and facilitate the negotiation of solutions that they are comfortable with. In the peer mediation program, selected student leaders are trained to mediate conflict among their peers. However, schoolteachers and staff members are also trained mediators and actively supervise the students' conflict mediation and facilitation processes. The goal of the peer mediation program is to introduce students and school personnel to the principles and practices of negotiated and inclusive conflict resolution programs.

Peer mediation is a new approach to conflict resolution and a mechanism for holding students accountable for behaviors that violate school rules and policies. Peer mediation programs help schools reduce the need for school suspension, expulsion, and juvenile justice system involvement in school misconduct. These programs help students with character building and the development of leadership and prosocial skills. Furthermore, students who participate in peer mediation training and programs develop a sense of empowerment and are likely to acquire useful and lifelong traits, such as integrity, honesty, and compassion. Student participants in the peer mediation program are also likely to acquire the values of responsibility, both to self and others. Students that participate in peer mediation programs develop more capacity for empathy. They also develop active listening skills and problem-solving techniques. They are also more likely to learn the effective way to express their emotions and also how to empower other participants to take ownership of the process of mediation and the issues at stake. Through the program, students develop critical thinking, problem-solving, and active citizenship skills, which are valuable in our multicultural world. Moreover, they also develop the necessary skills to resolve conflicts on their own.

Schools that employ peer mediation as their primary or alternative programs of conflict resolution are likely to increase communication among parents, teachers, administrators, and students. The program creates opportunities for the schools, parents, guardians, and the community to collaborate and share valuable ideas and resources in the upbringing of their children.

WHAT IS PEER MEDIATION?

Peer mediation is a structured and interactive conflict resolution program in a school setting. Peer mediation provides a platform for students of the same age cohort to assemble to mediate disputes between two or more people. Like the restorative justice principle that underpins it, peer mediation is both a process and a program. The purpose is to get students to resolve their problems on their own. Mediators do not impose a resolution on the disputants but rather facilitate a win-win resolution that is satisfactory to both parties in the dispute. Peer mediation is voluntary and provides an alternative to school disciplinary measures. Peer mediators are authorized to mediate on a wide array of disputes. Trained mediators assist the disputants in defining and clarifying the issues at stake. To facilitate the process of conflict resolution, mediators have the techniques to assist the disputants in exploring other perspectives and interests that will help them reach an agreement that they are satisfied with. As Hansberry and Hansberry (2018, p. 7) have observed, when peer mediation is "done well, peer mediator programs increase a climate of care and cooperation in schoolyards."

Trained mediators get to appreciate the value of active participation by disputants in negotiating a solution that is agreeable to all stakeholders. Students trained in peer mediation arrange a meeting in a private, safe place to mediate disputes between two or more students. Mediation is a negotiated process. Mediators employ dialogue, empathy, active listening, and persuasive techniques to get the disputants to open up and speak frankly about the issues they are concerned about. Participation in the peer mediation program is voluntary. All participants in the peer mediation program must enter into a confidentiality agreement. The mediator and the disputants are the only ones who are privy to what transpires during the mediation sessions. Students trained in negotiation techniques and specialized communication support assist other students in resolving their disputes in a peaceful manner. Schools may choose to either nominate capable and willing students to be trained in peer mediation or train every student in peer mediation techniques.

Peer mediation is party centered. This is because the focus of the conflict mediation process is the promotion and protection of the interests, rights, and needs of the participants. All the parties involved in the dispute actively participate in the search for a resolution that is acceptable to them with the guidance of the mediator. The mediator is a trained neutral individual and must demonstrate impartiality throughout the process. Again, the mediator is a trained facilitator applying a variety of techniques to guide the mediation process. The mediator also manages the interaction between the disputants, ensuring that the communication is open, respectful, and honest. The mediator evaluates the issues and the process to make sure all parties adhere to the relevant norms. However, he or she must refrain from prescribing solutions to the disputants. The mediator must allow for the open airing of relevant grievances and a decision must be reached through a consensus.

School Climate Survey

Before introducing the peer mediation program in a school, some groundwork must be done to ascertain the needs and resources that are available in the school. It is important to examine the school's administrative data about the number of school rule violations and the school's response, such as punishments meted out before and after the implementation of the peer mediation program. A survey of school staff, faculty, and students should be conducted to appraise their familiarity with the school's discipline policies and their knowledge about how recently and often some of those policies have been broken. It is also important to find out from members of the school community how they feel about the school's response to policy violations by students. The survey should also ascertain their perception of the fairness and effectiveness of the school's response to policy infractions.

The school climate survey should also measure how negative or positive student-to-student and teacher-to-student interactions are before and after the introduction of the peer mediation programs. The survey should measure the perceptions of the school community, teachers, students, administrators, and parents regarding the prevailing culture of discipline, kindness, respect, and caring in the school. A video or observation of the interactions between students on the one hand and between teachers and students on the other will provide valuable information about the culture of learning in the school. Such a study must be carried out before and after the implementation of the peer mediation program to understand if the climate of learning has improved for the better or not and if additional intervention is warranted.

Conflicts Handled by Peer Mediators

The school peer mediators are authorized to handle a variety of conflicts that may occur within the school community. Participation in the peer mediation process is voluntary. And the disputants must be willing and interested in participating in the process. Peer mediators are, however, not authorized to handle certain cases, such as sexual assault, drug abuse, weapons possession, and other felonies. Such serious cases are referred to the school authorities who handle them or refer them to law enforcement agencies in line with school policies. The following are the types of cases handled by peer mediators—namely, bullying, both physical and on social media, and fights. Conflicts arising from relationships and harassment are common in the school community and are handled through the peer mediation process. Other disputes that are handled by the school peer mediation programs include gossip and rumor-mongering, vandalism and stealing, racial and gang confrontations, and arguments and fights originating from sports, classroom, and other school activities. Truancy by students is also ideal for peer mediation.

GUIDELINES FOR PEER MEDIATION

The mediator provides the following explanation to the disputants at the beginning of the mediation session:

- The mediator reminds the disputants that participation in the mediation proceedings is voluntary.
- The mediator's role is the facilitation of the process; the mediator does not make any decisions on behalf of the disputants.
- The mediator reaffirms his or her neutrality and does not take sides or make determinations about who is right or wrong.
- The disputants are reminded that they have a chance to present their perspectives on the matter without interruption.
- All parties to the conflict must start by introducing themselves.
- The student litigants must agree not to engage in name-calling.
- The disputants must commit to resolving the conflict.
- The disputants must also agree not to interrupt the other person when he or she is speaking.
- The disputants must also agree to honestly present their cases as much as possible.
- All parties to the dispute must also agree to abide by any resolution reached and comply with any demands resulting from the resolution.
- All participants in the mediation must comply with confidentiality.
- After each disputant presents his or her case, the opposing party is asked to repeat the story to show that he or she fully understands the other person's position. The understanding of what the other party is saying is not the same as agreeing with the interpretation of the other person for the purposes of the mediation.

The Benefits of Peer Mediation

Peer mediation in schools is not a new concept. Many schools have been known to have organized students to address conflicts that may have arisen in their day-to-day interactions with varying results. According to available data, some of the schools that have experimented with peer mediation programs have many positive things to say about peer mediation. It is important to note that the interest in peer mediation is just beginning to receive attention; hence, there are few studies published that have evaluated peer mediation programs. Nonetheless, the following are some of the identified benefits of peer mediation from the evaluation studies of peer mediation programs in recent times.

Effective Resolution of Conflicts

Many evaluation studies undertaken to assess the benefits of peer mediation, although a good number of them are anecdotal, show that students were effective in resolving their conflicts. The studies undertaken to assess the benefits of peer mediation show that the student participants, teachers, school administrators, and participating parents were happy that the conflicts were effectively resolved for good.

One reason conflicts are effectively resolved through peer mediation for good to the satisfaction of all stakeholders is because the peer mediation process allows for the open hearing of all grievances, including the dispute that precipitated the conflict resolution meeting.

Students Learn Valuable Life Skills

In addition to their satisfaction with the outcome of peer mediation, student participants also acquire essential life skills, such as conflict resolution, effective communication, and the ability to generate and evaluate alternative solutions to their problems. Furthermore, through the peer mediation process, students learn how to coexist with others, including those they disagree with; they learn empathy and are more likely to understand the consequences of their actions. The conflict resolution and leadership skills the students learn through real-life peer mediation experiences are easily transferred to life as adults outside the school community. These skills are essential for success in today's global economy.

Peer Mediation Provides a Learning Opportunity

Peer mediation is an instrument for teaching students relevant knowledge and skills for resolving interpersonal conflicts. Cohen (2005) observes that students employ prosocial methods of conflict resolution, which emphasize fairness, empathy, and mutual benefit principles. In other words, students get to appreciate that violence, application of brute force, and intimidation are counterproductive and unacceptable in the school environment.

Empowerment of Students

Not all knowledge and skills are easily transferred through the traditional teaching method. Social skills, such as conflict resolution and specialized human relations training, are more effectively acquired through practice. Students trained in peer mediation put the idea to practice by resolving conflicts that arise among them. Students learn responsibility, empathy, negotiation, and tolerance through practice. Students who experience peer mediation training and practice are likely to change the way they view aggression, bonding, and sense of responsibility. As Costello et al. (2010) have suggested, when students are actively engaged in resolving their conflicts, they also take ownership of both the process and the outcome. They also suggest that the strong relationship and bonds engendered through the conflict resolution process also have positive effects on the students' academic development and performance. The introduction of peer mediation in schools does not eliminate school disciplinary measures, and students are well aware of that. Students know that if they fail to resolve their conflicts through the peer mediation processes, school authorities can still invoke and implement the school disciplinary policies.

Enhancement of Self-Esteem

Students who participate in peer mediation, and especially those who assist in resolving conflicts, get a sense of having contributed in significant ways to the operation of the school. Student peer mediators have a sense of pride and accomplishment in having contributed in meaningful ways to making an important difference in the lives of their peers. This enhances their practical intelligence and self-esteem. Furthermore, the students get to have greater insight into school policies and the values that underpin them. This makes them take ownership and feel a sense of partnership with the school administrators. Hansberry and Hansberry (2018, p. 7) citing Werner (1984) note that people derive "lasting positive emotional changes" when they render help to others. They state that "many cultures share common teachings that humans can reach heights of happiness, fulfilment and connection to others (that we seek) when they commit to a way of living that maintains a focus on being helpful to others." Above all, the skills developed through the peer mediation program will enhance the students' social skills and serve them later in life. The peer mediation program will likely reduce the disproportionate minority student contact with the juvenile justice system.

More Time for Learning

One major benefit of peer mediation is that it saves the school a lot of time and, therefore, creates more time for teaching and learning. Empowering students to mediate conflicts means the teachers and school administrators are less involved in mediating and disciplining students. Teachers and the school administration save a lot of time from reduced suspension, expulsion, and breaking up fights. Again, there is a reduction in conflicts with the peer mediation programs. This means that students and teachers are less distracted and more likely to focus their time on the important school business of teaching and learning. The transformational values that result from the active involvement of the school community in conflict resolution means teachers too learn affective and effective responses to students' behavior that may not conform with school rules and policies, according to Costello et al. (2009). Peer mediation also helps bring about a reduction in truancy and school rule infraction. It is also believed that the peer mediation program will reduce school disciplinary problems and improve schools' academic performance.

SELECTING STUDENT MEDIATORS

Schools can choose to train each student to be a peer mediator. They can also select a few to be trained mediators for practical purposes, as it would cost enormous amounts of money and time to train every student. Besides, not every student will show an interest in being a mediator. Nonetheless, the knowledge and skills from the peer mediation training are valuable and should be taught to every student, even if they do not desire to mediate cases for others. However, there is the danger of selecting only outgoing and popular students to be peer mediators. It is important to diversify for full benefit, including those thought of as troublesome. The difficult students who often get into trouble are those who bring good insight into the process. As Hansberry and Hansberry (2018, p.10) in support note, "*Troubled* students reinvent themselves through involvement in programs that place them in positions of caring responsibility. It is often the case that young people only start to reflect on their own habitual responses to conflict when they become involved with others in a pastoral sense" (emphasis in original).

Their suggestion is that school authorities should take the risk in selecting students from diverse backgrounds and personalities to be trained for peer mediation. The mediators ideally should reflect the school demographics, such as race, ethnicity, gender, sexual orientation, and academic ability. The selection process should be open and widely publicized. Students can be referred by other students and/ or teachers and administrators. Students interested in being trained as peer mediators can also volunteer through self-referral. Nonetheless, Hansberry and Hansberry (2018, p. 15) argue that the ideal mediators must possess the following qualities:

- Kind and caring to others
- Fair and understanding—doesn't take sides
- A good listener—lets others talk
- Can stay calm in tricky moments
- Can be trusted
- Reliable—shows up when they are needed
- Confident and friendly around younger students

DISCUSSION QUESTIONS

1. What concepts and practices of peer mediation reduce student-to-student and student-to-teacher conflicts?
2. How do students' negotiation and collaborative problem-solving skills and values help to reduce conflict?
3. What peer meditation methods promote caring, social, emotional, responsible, and supportive learning environments?
4. What peer meditation methods enhance student-to-student and student-to-teacher relationships?
5. What peer meditation methods inculcate students' values of respect, fairness, empathy, nonviolence, trust, tolerance, and inclusive negotiation and mediation skills?

REFERENCES

Cohen, R. (2005). *Students restoring conflict: Peer mediation in schools* (2nd ed.). Good Year Books, Culver City, CA.

Costello, B., Wachtel, J., & Wachtel, T. (2009). *The restorative practices handbook for teachers, disciplinarians and administrators: Building a culture of community in schools.* Bethlehem, Pennsylvania: International Institute for Restorative Practices.

Costello, B., Wachtel, J., & Wachtel, T. (2010). *Restorative circles in schools: Building community and enhancing learning—a practical guide for educators.* Bethlehem, Pennsylvania: International Institute for Restorative Practices.

Hansberry, B., & Hansberry, C. L. (2018). *How to do restorative peer mediation in your school.* Philadelphia, PA: Jessica Kingsley Publishers.

Thorsborne, M. & Blood, P. (2013). *Implementing restorative practices in schools: A practical guide to transforming school communities.* Philadelphia, PA: Jessica Kingsley Publishers.

Wachtel, T., O'Connell, T., & Wachtel, B. (2010). *Restorative justice conferencing: Real justice and the conferencing handbook.* Pipersville, Pennsylvania: International Institute for Restorative Practices.

Werner, E. E. (1984). Resilient children. *Young Children, 40,* 68–72.

CHAPTER NINE

Popular School Violence Programs

Katalin Parti

READING OBJECTIVES

- Get familiar with the common components of the school-based anti-bullying programs of today.
- Examine anti-bullying programs applied in the United States and all over the world.
- Review evidence of success listed and analyzed through examples.
- Explain the recommendation of the components of the law and school protocols.
- See the weak points in school violence programs and develop critical thinking about them.

OVERVIEW

The chapter gives an overview of five popular school violence programs that contain an anti-bullying component running in the United States today: Olweus Bullying Prevention Program (OBPP), Positive Action, Second Step, and Second Step: Student Success Through Prevention middle school program (Committee for Children), Steps to Respect (Committee for Children), and KiVa, an anti-bullying program developed in Finland.

These five programs were selected because all of them are in use in the United States (among other countries).

These programs are characterized by the following features:

- They look back on many years or decades of *experience*.
- Several *impact studies* linked to the programs provide evidence of the operation of the programs in practice, their applicability, and the less successful program elements.

- They are school-based intervention programs with a *reliable* (experimental[1] or quasi-experimental[2]) *group design.* Each program reports data in the statistical format necessary to calculate effect size (e.g., mean, standard deviation, group size, percentage). Therefore, their effect and success are evidenced.
- They are also *implemented internationally*, and they have been successfully adapted in several countries and different continents (e.g., Europe, America, Australia).
- They contain *components developed for bullying situations*: curriculum, training, and other sensitization tools for school staff and students.
- They are complex program packages aimed at the whole community—teachers, other school staff members, students, parents—based on the *whole-school approach.* (This is essential because only those programs managed to achieve a positive impact so far, that were aimed at the whole school and the community even beyond the school; Smith, Schneider, Smith, & Ananiadou, 2004.)
- They are complex module systems approaching the targeted population groups with *different methods*, containing teacher training, parental meetings, student curricula, and sensitizing conferences addressed to the community that comes into regular contact with students.
- They use a *terminology* widely accepted in international literature on the topic. The definition of bullying used by the reviewed programs can be described as follows. "*The definition of school bullying includes several key elements: (1) physical, verbal, or psychological attack or intimidation that is intended to cause fear, distress, or harm to the victim; (2) an imbalance of power (psychological or physical) with a more powerful child (or children) oppressing less powerful ones; (3) and repeated incidents between the same children over a prolonged period of time*" (Farrington, 1993; Olweus, 1993; Ttofi & Farrington, 2011). Consequently, it is not considered bullying when two persons of equal power (physical, psychological, or verbal) or in equal positions of power come into a one-off conflict. Children are given the following definition in questionnaires based on the Olweus Bully/Victim Questionnaire: "*(It is bullying when) ... one child is repeatedly exposed to harassment and attacks from one or several other children. Harassment and attacks may be, for example, shoving or hitting the other one, calling him/her names or making jokes about him/her, leaving him/her outside the group, taking his/her things, or any other behavior meant to hurt the other one. It is not bullying, when two students with equal strength or equal power have a fight, or when someone is occasionally teased, but it is bullying, when the feelings of one and same student are intentionally and repeatedly hurt*" (Olweus, 1991; 2001). A further attribute of school bullying is that it occurs on the *premises* of the school, or *outside*—on the way to or from school (Ttofi & Farrington, 2011). It might occur between students after school, the effect of which is felt at school—in the form of ruining school climate, disrupting the peaceful learning atmosphere, or even weakening the cohesion of a smaller community (learning group, class).

Characteristically, these programs include prevention and intervention elements or a combination of the two: they exert their influence through general sensitization and individual skills building. Within that, they put more emphasis on proactive, preventive techniques than on reactive, subsequent response. Consequently, they contain education of not only the bully and the victim but also the bystanders, children standing up for each other, and, in some cases, peer mentor training as well.

The programs consist of several components on various levels. A typical element is the classroom curriculum, which may range from a few sessions to a systematic offer of classes for a whole semester. The written curriculum of classes is sometimes supported by video spots, and in some cases (KiVa), online video games help students understand the incidents. In addition to the informative, sensitizing classes held for students, direct training for educators also appears as a compulsory program element, which may be complemented by indirect training for a trainer certificate (train the trainer). Educators with such a certificate are entitled to hold trainings for other educators. The programs also include parent meetings and school conferences. The programs support the teaching staff with complete protocols for the resolution of cases and appropriate and recommend responses. All written materials for the programs (curriculum, black lines, procedural protocols, reporting forms, information materials for parents, etc.) are available and can usually be downloaded for a fee from the program websites. Programs might also include improved playground supervision and a whole-school anti-bullying policy, disciplinary (but nonpunitive) methods, classroom rules, and cooperative group work.

RESEARCH ON SCHOOL-BASED VIOLENCE PROGRAMS

Of the meta-analyses evaluating anti-bullying programs (Smith et al., 2004; Lösel & Beelman, 2003; Merrell, Isava, Gueldner, & Scott, 2008; Ttofi & Farrington, 2011; Evans, Frazer, & Cotter, 2014; Yeager, Fong, Lee, & Espelage, 2015), the most rigorous so far is the Ttofi-Farrington study (Ttofi & Farrington, 2011), aggregating 44 different program evaluations based on the procedure of the Campbell Collaboration Systematic Review (Campbell Collaboration, 2014), which compared the findings of randomized clinical trials. It established that the analyzed programs based on the procedure of appropriately documented, randomized controlled trials reduced the incidence of bullying by an average of 20% to 23% and victimization by 17% to 20%. The reduction of victimization indices showed a correlation with the following program elements: disciplinary (nonpunitive) methods, parent training/meetings, use of videos, cooperative group work, and duration and intensity of the program. In comparison, to reduce the indices of perpetration, the following program elements were necessary: improved playground supervision, teacher training, classroom management, classroom rules, whole-school anti-bullying policy, school conferences, information for parents, and cooperative group work. As we see, the relatively profound implementation of program elements involving the whole-school community is necessary to reduce perpetration.

It has also become clear that the sole use of an anti-bullying curriculum shows no significant correlation with either perpetration or victimization (Ttofi & Farrington, 2011). The **different program elements** can change the school climate and improve bullying indices in an **interdependent and synergistic way**.

Programs focusing on older children (above the age of 11) achieved better results than programs aimed at younger children (Ttofi & Farrington, 2011). Admittedly, according to Smith and his colleagues, this is possible because Ttofi and Farrington applied between-program comparisons instead of within-program comparisons in their meta-analysis. Any one program, however, is aimed at several **age groups** and contains age-specific components. For this reason, the effects of age-specific program components need to be assessed for each age group within the same program. It has been proven that if the comparison is made *between* the age groups, then the most positive effect can be achieved at 6 to 11 years of age (Smith, Salmivalli, & Cowie, 2012).

Anti-bullying programs introduced in the United States rely on the elements and methods of the OBPP for the assessment, prevention, and management of the phenomenon. In contrast to the original OBPP implemented in Norway on a nationwide sample, these research projects produced **statistically not significant, in certain cases negative but at best mixed, results**. Evans and his colleagues, who compared the findings of research published between 2011 and 2014 following the meta-analysis of Ttofi and Farrington (Evans et al., 2014) established that the programs implemented in Europe may have produced better results because the assessed population and the sample taken were more homogenous.

DESCRIPTION OF THE PROGRAMS, SCHOOL PRACTICES, AND POLICIES

OBPP

Whole-school anti-bullying programs were inspired by the first study of Dan Olweus in Bergen, Norway (Bergen Study). Olweus (1991) introduced a multilayered approach, which contained different intervention components for elementary, middle, and high school individuals (aged 8 to 18), classes, and schools. Earlier research mostly disregarded the heterogeneity of the population. Olweus avoided the distortions of heterogeneous samples by using a hierarchical model: He took the attributes of the sample in consideration based on single classes, schools, and age cohorts. Besides OBPP, KiVa is the only other program using this approach (Salmivalli, Kaukiainen, & Voeten, 2005).

Olweus believes that assessment is important at three levels:

1. Serious talks with the perpetrators and the victims—*individual level*
2. Classroom discussions—*classroom level*
3. Staff meetings—*school level*

He used a cohort-longitudinal design with time-lagged comparisons of the grades. With this design, after the intervention, students were compared with students of the same grades before the intervention. The advantage of this method is that control schools are not needed to measure the effect.

The program was successfully adapted in the whole of Norway and elsewhere in Scandinavia and other Western European countries. Nothing speaks more about the program's success than the fact that, controlled for age and grades, self-reported bully and self-reported victim indices fell by 50%. Indices of antisocial behavior (vandalism, truancy, conflicts with the police, intoxication in public) also fell, and the program achieved an improvement in the school atmosphere. The New National Initiative Against Bullying started as the continuation of the Bergen Study in 2001, as a result of which bullying victimization fell by 34% by the end of the 12 months following the introduction of the intervention (Olweus & Limber, 2010). After the initial success, the effectiveness of OBPP decreased, but it still achieves by far the best results of any anti-bullying program applied.

In the United States, the program was first introduced in the early 1990s in California. Since then, all states use it to some degree. The most important evaluations were carried out in South Carolina; Seattle, Washington; California; Philadelphia, Pennsylvania; and the state of Pennsylvania. In the California assessment, the program achieved a drop in the prevalence of self-reported bullying and antisocial behaviors, but it did not result in a drop in self-reported victimization and a statistically significant improvement in the school atmosphere. The South Carolina program brought statistically significant results 12 months after its introduction, but no such results could be identified after the second year of the program. The Seattle study did not generate any identifiable results in relation to physical and relational victimization. It must be noted that both types of victimization decreased among white intervention students, but no substantive results were seen among students of other ethnic backgrounds (Bauer, Lozano, & Rivara, 2007).

The program, therefore, was not as successful in the United States as it was in its country of origin. The reasons for this may be (1) the lower degree of program implementation; (2) lack of school resources; (3) different degrees of social responsibility—one of the most important values of OBPP cannot be transposed into the power-centered and personality-oriented culture of the United States; (4) balance between cultural effectiveness and fidelity to the program's design is sometimes difficult to attain; (5) basic level of training of teachers is different from Norway (characteristics of training); (6) education is more practice oriented in the United States; (7) student, staff, and administrator turnover is greater at U.S. schools—especially in big cities; (8) the activities of the teachers participating in the program, of the school management, and of the school coordinating committee are not synchronized (Limber, 2011).

During the assessment of the effects of prevention programs implemented in low-income urban areas, it was established that educators mainly apply the reactive, rather than the proactive, intervention elements. These strategies react exclusively to physical bullying, disobedience, and open disrespect (Talbott, Celinska, & Simpson, 2002). The OBPP does not offer special solutions against bullying for impoverished communities in the United States (e.g., African American and Hispanic teenage parents; Hong, 2009). There are difficulties integrating parents into the programs in such an environment (e.g., they are unable to supervise the school progress of their children because of their long working hours; Gross, Sambrook, & Fogg, 1999). As a result, teachers have a greater role to play in the social education of children in low-income neighborhoods. However, they fulfill this role without special training and preparation (e.g., their basic training does not prepare them for the empathy needed for "problematic" children or the appropriate communication to use with them). It has to be noted that it is not only anti-bullying programs but also empathy research projects that are not giving educators suitable support (McMahon, Wernsman, & Parnes, 2006). For example, established that empathy programs only focus on the white middle-class population, which is probably the least in need of such help (Hong, 2009).

OBPP did not work that well in the US as: 1) the school coordinating committee that is essential to meet regularly in order to create customized classroom rules and individual level intervention protocols, could not manage to meet regularly (Limber, Nation, Tracy, Melton, & Flerx, 2004). Many public schools were underserved and understaffed to fulfill this requirement. 2) On the other hand, motivation was frequently missing to maintain the program for the minimally required 4 years (Black & Jackson, 2007). 3) Community involvement requires enormous amount of energy and time, that was another critical issue that resulted in the attrition of participating classes and schools (Limber et al., 2004).

Positive Action

Positive Action System Inc. was developed in 1983 by Carol Gerber Allred, PhD, who was a teacher and administrator at a public school. Today, altogether, five million students at 15,000 schools across all states in the United States use this scientifically founded method, which is based on several impact studies and relies on the involvement of the whole school. It is a comprehensive social-emotional and character development program whose aim is to develop the basic skills of children to reduce their deviances (e.g., truancy, bullying, drug abuse), to act against early sexual activity, to increase tolerance for others, and to develop the skills needed for cooperative work based on the methods of social-emotional learning. The program is grounded in theories of self-concept, self-esteem enhancement theory, and consistent with integrative and socio-ecologic theories of health behaviors (Lewis et al., 2013). Detailed manuals are provided to the teachers for the curricula. By illustrating the think-act-feel process, educators show the students how their thoughts lead to actions and what emotions they trigger. Taking responsibility for one's actions, avoiding blaming others, and exhibiting self-knowledge all contribute to achieving a better performance. The developers consider it important that in the interest of achieving lasting and profound effects, not only "problem" classes but all students of the school should participate in the program, which follows children from kindergarten through the last grade of high school (curriculum for Pre-K–12 students). In addition to the students, educators, parents, and the community also participate in the program (school climate program, family kit, community kit). Supplementary curricula are available for the basic package, which covers such topics as bullying, drug abuse, school counseling, and conflict management (elementary bullying prevention supplement kit, elementary and secondary drug education supplement kit, counselor's kit, conflict resolution kit). The program components can be chosen and combined freely at the level of individuals, small groups, and classrooms. Hence educators have more freedom in implementation, but the degree of implementation is more difficult to control. It must be noted that among all examined programs, Positive Action is the only one containing a separate module for family and community engagement (family kit, community kit). These modules describe how parents and members of the community (nongovernmental organizations, activists, individuals, health and welfare agencies, media, law enforcement, and judicial entities) can be involved in the program and, therefore, indirectly contribute to creating a more peaceful and supportive school climate.

According to the findings of evaluative analyses, students of intervention schools admitted less drug abuse in self-report questionnaires than students of control schools. Levels of self-reported violent behavior also fell in the experimental schools, which was confirmed by the teacher reports. The long-term program effects have also been confirmed: The prevalence of "problem behaviors" (such as drug abuse, violent behavior, and early sexual activity) dropped considerably with children who participated in the intervention for at least 3 to 4 years as opposed to students whose participation was shorter. In the same way, the decline of school grades, the number of suspensions, and days of absence were reduced significantly, and basic skills (literacy, arithmetic) improved after at least 3 years of intervention. (Beets et al., 2009; Snyder et al., 2010; Snyder, Vuchinich, Acock, Washburn, & Flay, 2012; Washburn et al., 2011). It can be established that in the case of program elements intended to develop basic skills (e.g., literacy, reading tests, arithmetic) and the reduction of violent incidents, *elementary* schools showed a great development of statistical significance (Flay & Allred, 2003).

Second Step

Second Step is a social-emotional-learning-focused program that develops conflict management and conflict prevention skills based on the risk and protective factors of involvement in bullying. The program has been applied by more than 32,000 schools since 1987 in the United States. Since 2004, about four million students and two million adults have participated in the program. It offers a curriculum from pre-kindergarten through eighth grade, with one class per week for 23 weeks per academic year. The curriculum is age specific and is based on empathy training, impulse control, problem solving, and anger management. There are further modules on sexual harassment, substance abuse, and violence and bullying for middle schools. In addition to the curriculum, an online training and detailed instructions for the implementation are offered. The aim is to integrate the curriculum into the daily routine of the school. Second Step, developed by the Committee for Children, is founded on Albert Bandura's social cognitive theory (Bandura, 1977) and manages problems using the method of social and emotional learning. Lessons are skills based; students receive cueing, coaching, and suggestions for improvement of performance. Learning is aided by video exercises, interactive tasks, and homework. A special intervention is developed for middle schools (Second Step: Student Success Through Prevention).

Second Step has been evaluated in multiple randomized and quasi-experimental studies (two randomized control trials and two experimental). Students were followed over the course of up to 2 years. The students of intervention schools participating in the Second Step: Student Success Through Prevention program (in the states of Kansas and Illinois) showed statistically significant results in the reduction of physical bullying in relation to the program, but with other problems targeted—such as bullying victimization, homophobic name-calling, sexual harassment—the program was *not* successful (Espelage, Low, Polanin, & Brown, 2013; 2015). It is remarkable that the positive results could be established only in the first year of intervention. Later, the rate of improvement fell, or it was not possible to identify a statistically significant correlation between the changes and the program effect. Frey and her colleagues assessed the antisocial behavior index and its changes in elementary and middle schools. The evaluation in this case only showed a statistically significant improvement in the first year of the intervention: the incidence of antisocial behaviors dropped in verifiable correlation with the program but only in children whose antisocial baseline ratings were high (Frey, Nolen, Van Schoiack-Edstrom, & Hirschstein, 2005). This was established by research in relation to the baseline assessments of aggression management and prevention programs in schools based on social-emotional learning, and the programs require further revision and development for their adaptation to moderately violent children showing behavior disruptive to the community (Frey et al., 2005).

Steps to Respect

Steps to Respect: A Bullying Prevention Program is based on the socio-ecological model of bullying developed for students in third to sixth grade by the Committee for Children. It was implemented first in 2001, and since then, approximately 6.72 million schoolchildren have participated in the program in 3,600 institutions in the 50 states of the United States. Its basic assumption is that bullying is a complex phenomenon that appears in peer groups and is influenced by several different factors at the level of the school, the peer group, and the individual (Swearer, Espelage, Vaillancourt, & Hymel, 2010). It focuses on creating a positive school atmosphere, which the teachers have to confirm in students. There are teacher and staff trainings; the school has to introduce an effective disciplinary policy; the students need to be constantly monitored and taught prosocial and assertive behaviors and how they should intervene when they witness bullying (*individual characteristics improvement*). The program develops positive interactions between children and helps form healthy social relationships (*social context*).

The program is implemented in three phases: (1) the school conducts a baseline survey with the children to assess bullying and victimization and to map out the policies and procedures in place at the school for the prevention and management of bullying; (2) all adults working at the school participate in trainings, where they learn how to quickly identify, manage, and prevent bullying and learn how to coach students to avoid bullying and to intervene effectively; (3) children are sensitized in classroom lessons for 12 to 14 weeks and given resolution schemes for practical use in the management of bullying. The school-level and parental packages describe how anti-bullying policies should be ideally structured. It puts a great emphasis on fidelity monitoring (e.g., teachers have to fill in an online program implementation log every week about the level of attention of the students in class, their dedication to the curriculum, and behaviors disruptive to the attention of the class; Brown, Low, Smith, & Haggerty, 2011).

The major distinguishing features of Steps to Respect are as follows:

- The effects of the single components (proximal or distal) are assessed separately during program evaluation.
- Bullying prevalence, victimization, and the bystander phenomenon, along with other antisocial behaviors, are assessed by various assessment tools (student self-report, teacher rating scale, teacher observations) and produce controlled and valid results.
- Innovative tools (e.g., playground observation, coaching of students) are tested for assessing and teaching the rules of social relations and empathic behavior.

- Program fidelity is ensured by using high-level monitoring and detailed program implementation guides.
- Options and tools citing specific examples for the practical application of the results are also provided.

KiVa

KiVa is the most recent of the programs reviewed here. In 2006, the Finnish Ministry of Education and Culture contracted the University of Turku Department of Psychology and the Centre for Learning Research to develop a comprehensive anti-bullying program for Finnish primary schools and high schools (students in grades 1 to 9) and carry out its evaluation study. The first test phase of the program started in the academic year 2007/2008, with the intervention involving students in grades 4 to 6. KiVa is an acronym, an abbreviation of kusaamista vastaan ("against bullying" in Finnish). The program is used nationwide in Finland.

KiVa is based on the theoretical assumptions of research on the social status of violent children, of children who become bullies in general, and on bullying as a group activity (Kärnä et al., 2011b). Like Second Step, it relies on Bandura's social cognitive theory in the analysis of group dynamics and behavioral norms in groups (Bandura, 1989).

KiVa, incorporating the experience gained from OBPP, consists of *universal actions* targeting all students through lessons and virtual learning environments (e.g., anti-bullying computer games) and *indicated actions* tackling acute bullying cases. The student lessons are taught by the classroom teachers following a strict schedule during school hours. In addition, KiVa posters, parents' guidance, and highly visible vests for teachers supervising recess time are included. The virtual learning environment provides anti-bullying computer games (for the primary school) and an online forum "KiVa Street" (for the secondary school). The program is quite intensive, and the implementation takes one entire school year (from mid-August to the end of May, 9 months; Kärnä et al., 2011a).

Very few interventions contain a special impact analysis on subgroups, such as popular bullies or mixed-role students (i.e., bully victims). KiVa is an exception to that, as it examines the behavior of bully victims in detail, as well as how the anti-bullying program affects their behavior. Yang and Salmivalli (2015) found that the program is not only effective in reducing the prevalence of bully and victim behavior but also that of bully victim behavior. The prevalence of bully victims in intervention schools, in comparison with control schools, dropped by 8% and 41% when identified by self-reports and peer reports. Controlling for gender, school level, and pretest bullying/victimization status, the odds of being a bully victim after an intervention year were 1.51 (self-reports) and 1.63 (peer reports) times higher for a student in a control school in comparison with a student in an intervention school (Yang & Salmivalli, 2015). They also examined what role the motivation levels of teachers, their attitudes, and their conviction to the program's success played in increasing the program's effect. Teachers who clearly and actively stood for anti-bullying norms were likely to strengthen the normative goal of potential bullies and victims. Teachers' efforts cross-sectionally correlated with a higher level of peer-reported bullying in the first year of evaluation, but over time, they correlated with drop-in, peer-reported bullying (Veenstra, Lindenberg, Huitsing, Sainio, & Salmivalli, 2014). In another analysis, they examined the effect of appreciation by the community on popular bullies. The activities of perpetrators of medium and low popularity in intervention schools fell because of the program, but very popular bullies were not responsive (Garandeau, Lee, & Salmivalli, 2014). This result is particularly worrying, as anti-bullying programs are mostly aimed at victims and communities (e.g., mobilizing bystanders, exercise for supporting victims), but they do not offer alternatives to popular children for maintaining their social position after they stop bullying (Garandeau et al., 2014).

The KiVa program is found more effective in grades 1 to 6 than in grades 7 to 9 (Kärnä et al., 2011b; 2013). The background of this result—which is in contrast with the meta-analysis of Ttofi and Farrington (2011)—has not been examined in detail in evaluations. Researchers, however, suspect that the reason for these discrepancies is rooted in sample size: KiVa is a nationwide sample. It is also worth noting that the effect of KiVa was slightly more expressed on victimization than perpetration and caused it to drop more significantly. The reason for this may be that it is easier to teach protection mechanisms to victims than to convince perpetrators that what they are doing does not pay off.

The advantages of KiVa, compared to the other programs described here are as follows:

- Extended documentation is available. Manuals, school policies, research theory and background, recruitment of schools, evaluation, and results are well documented and widely available. Continuous support (consultation) and the motivation to maintain the degree of implementation are ensured through monitoring of schools. If educators receive continuous feedback telling them that their work is counted on in the program, then the consistency of the degree of implementation can be maintained (Kärnä et al., 2011b).
- Groups are evaluated several times. Beyond the usual indices—self-reported bully, self-reported victim, peer-reported bully, peer-reported victim— evaluations also include the examination of a third group, that of bully victims, comparison within grades, and conclusions based on the degree of implementation.
- Analysts of KiVa do not only deal with measuring victim prevalence but also highlight deeper correlations—for example, the bystander-group effect (i.e., how passive onlookers can be moved to step out of their bystander role, how notorious bullies can be influenced to follow norms, or how bullying

influences the general well-being of students) They also assess "predictor effects" to forecast future problem behaviors and to estimate trends and trend effects. This is based on a nationwide controlled trial and a longitudinal study.

- Using a thoroughly planned methodology, they carried out impact assessments to monitor the program effect in every age group.
- It gives implication ideas for policy and practice: proposals for practical implementation based on earlier experience and how results are best implemented in different policies (i.e., how it can be best coordinated with other school or crime prevention programs, how the results may be used in elaborating school anti-bullying policies).

JUVENILE JUSTICE AND POLICY IMPLICATIONS

We have seen how much extra effort is needed to make an anti-bullying program successful. It is not enough to maintain strict methodology or follow program manuals; there has to be commitment, sustainability, and fidelity to the program; high levels of motivation from the school staff and the director; cooperative teamwork from every target group involved (teachers, students, parents, community); low turnover; and good basic education of teachers, which helps them to better understand and easily adapt to the program's requirements. In addition, selected program elements might bring different levels of success to different socioeconomic populations and age groups.

After listing the required program elements in detail, let us have a look at juvenile justice and policy implications in general.

Hatzenbuehler and colleagues looked at the data to find out what common components school violence laws must have to prevent and repel bullying and cyberbullying successfully (Hatzenbuehler et al., 2015). The results suggest that local policies are an important element of a comprehensive strategy for preventing and managing peer bullying. Data on anti-bullying legislation was obtained from the U.S. Department of Education (DoE), which commissioned a systematic review of state law on school violence. Out of the key components identified, four broad categories were created: (1) purpose and definition of the law, (2) district policy development and review, (3) school district policy components (e.g., responsibilities for reporting bullying incidents), and (4) additional components (e.g., how policies are communicated). Policy variables were linked to state-by-state data from the national 2013 Youth Risk Behavior Surveillance Survey. Compliance with at least one DoE-recommended component in their anti-bullying laws was associated with lower rates of being bullied and cyberbullied among high school students (grades 9–12). In states with at least one recommended component in their laws, there was a 24% (95% CI, 15%–32%) reduction in reporting of bullying and a 20% (95% CI, 9%–29%) reduction in reporting of cyber-bullying (Hatzenbuehler et al., 2015). Three DoE recommendations were associated with decreased odds of perceived bullying and cyberbullying: (1) having a statement of scope, (2) having a description of prohibited behaviors, and (3) having requirements for school districts to develop and implement local policies.

What does each of these components mean in practice?

Schools must list the components and definitions of prohibited behaviors. *Anti-bullying laws have to be concrete in determining certain behaviors, behavior components, and outcomes (harm and damage caused) of behaviors in which the school has to act in its internal scope.* These are bullying and cyberbullying gateway behaviors, or even petty crimes where schools have their competent personnel with appropriate professional backgrounds (school counselor, guidance counselor, school psychologist, etc.). In their scope, schools have to deal with those acts that occurred on-campus and during school time as a golden rule. But a statement of scope *should cover the protocol to deal with off-campus and off-school behaviors as well* that disrupt the peaceful school climate. Consequently, schools must provide a list of behaviors with a serious outcome when police or other authorities (Department of Children and Family Services, other local child care services, etc.) have to be called, and so *the solution of the case has to be brought through an orchestrated effort of the school and the authorities (external scope).*

Furthermore, it is of utmost importance that *school districts identify, develop, and implement their policies to prevent and manage bullying. Local needs have to be identified*—prevalence and patterns of bullying and cyberbullying have to be measured, and responses have to be developed locally, according to the specific socioeconomic strata and the developmental and educational challenges of the students of the given school district.

SUMMARY

The core components of anti-bullying programs are class curriculum, training of educators, train-the-trainer modules, parent meetings, or school conferences. Programs might also include playground supervision, recommendations for whole-school anti-bullying policies, disciplinary (nonpunitive) methods, classroom rules, cooperative group work, and case resolutions. These components are applied in an interdependent and synergistic way.

Most programs function on two levels: individual and group (classroom/school). Some programs rely on social emotional learning and social cognitive theory and aim for better school performance in general. It is proven that improving school performance and reducing deviances, such as truancy and substance abuse, can enhance anti-bullying prevention.

According to meta-analyses, anti-bullying programs introduced after the OBPP—which achieved a significant drop in the prevalence of both bullies and victims—have led to contradictory, in some cases negative but at least mixed, results. Analysts believe that, besides the obvious social and economic differences of the population, several important flaws in methodology are to blame.

Programs perform differently at different age groups. In general, older children (11 years of age and above) react better, but, for example, at KiVa, pupils who are 6–11 years of age reacted the best to the program. Reasons can be tackled in the difference in program components and in the methodology.

Programs are not guaranteed to make an impact, even with the most thorough methodology, when they are applied for less than 3 to 4 years. Programs have to be time sustained. Also, in the interest of reliability and validity, data needs to be collected routinely and systematically over a long period within a set time frame.

Even though reaching out to parents is the most difficult aspect, their involvement in the program is necessary both to protect children's rights to privacy and program fidelity. The highest possible number of school staff members must be involved in the realization of the program. Committee involvement can also significantly improve the school climate.

Challenges of school violence programs lie in tackling group dynamics and targeting subgroups, such as highly popular pupils in the classroom.

Even if the school is prepared and methodology recommendations are strictly followed, introducing and maintaining an anti-bullying program requires much effort from the schools involved. School districts have to set up their statements of scope, make the list of prohibited behaviors transparent, and develop their own policies based on local needs and appropriate answers to them.

DISCUSSION QUESTIONS

1. What are the common components of the most well-known, school-based anti-bullying programs?
2. Mention some of the weak points of the anti-bullying programs described.
3. List some of the reasons anti-bullying programs need to be introduced somewhat differently.
4. What is the evidence of the success of anti-bullying programs?
5. What is recommended for school districts to achieve success in antiviolence efforts?

REFERENCES

Bandura, A. (1977). Self-efficacy: Toward a unifying theory of behavioral change. *Psychological Review, 84*, 191–215.

Bandura, A. (1989). Social cognitive theory. In R. Vasta (Ed.), *Annals of child development: Six theories of child development* (vol. 6, pp. 1–60). Greenwich, CT: JAI Press.

Bauer, N., Lozano, P., & Rivara, F. P. (2007). The effectiveness of the Olweus bullying prevention program in public middle schools: A controlled trial. *Journal of Adolescent Health, 40*(3), 266–274.

Beets, M. W., Flay, B. R., Vuchinich, S., Snyder, F. J., Acock, A., Li, K.-K., & Durlak, J. A. (2009). Use of a social and character development program to prevent substance use, violent behaviors, and sexual activity among elementary students in Hawaii. *American Journal of Public Health, 99*(8), 1438–1445.

Black, S. A., & Jackson, E. (2007). Using bullying incident density to evaluate the Olweus bullying prevention programme. *School Psychology International, 28*, 623–638.

Brown, E. C., Low, S., Smith, B. H., & Haggerty, K. P. (2011). Outcomes from a school-randomized controlled trial of Steps to respect: A bullying prevention program. *School Psychology Review, 40*(3), 423–443.

Campbell Collaboration. (2014). Campbell collaboration systematic reviews: Policies and guidelines (V 1.0). *Campbell Collaboration Systematic Reviews*. Retrieved from www.campbellcollaboration.org

Englander, K. E. (2013). *Bullying and cyberbullying: What every educator needs to know.* Cambridge, MA: Harvard Education Press.

Espelage, D. L., Low, S., Polanin, J. R., & Brown, E. (2013). The impact of middle school program to reduce aggression, victimization, and sexual violence. *Journal of Adolescent Health, 53*(2), 180–186.

Espelage, D. L., Low, S., Polanin, J. R. & Brown, E. C. (2015). Clinical trial of Second Step© middle-school program: Impact on aggression and victimization. *Journal of Applied Developmental Psychology, 37*(1), 52–63, https://doi.org/10.1016/j.appdev.2014.11.007

Evans, C.B.R., Frazer, M. W., & Cotter, K. L. (2014). The effectiveness of school-based bullying prevention programs: A systematic review. *Aggression and Violent Behaviour, 19*, 532–544.

Farrington, D. P. (1993). Understanding and preventing bullying. In M. Tonry (Ed.), *Crime and justice* (vol. 17, pp. 381–458). Chicago, IL: University of Chicago Press.

Flay, B. R. & Allred, C. G (2003). Long-term effects of the Positive Action program—A comprehensive, positive youth development program, *American Journal of Health Behavior, 27*(Supplement 1), S6-S21

Frey, K. S., Nolen, S. B., Van Schoiack-Edstrom, L. & Hirschstein, M. K. (2005). Effect of a school-based social-emotional competence program: Linking children's goals, attributions, and behavior. *Applied Developmental Psychology, 26*, 171–200.

Garandeau, C. F., Lee, I. A., & Salmivalli, C. (2014). Differential effects of the KiVa anti-bullying program on popular and unpopular bullies. *Journal of Applied Developmental*

Psychology, 35, 44–50. Retrieved from http://www.sciencedirect.com/science/article/pii/S0193397313000828

Gross, D., Sambrook, A., & Fogg, L. (1999). Behavior problems among young children in low-income urban day care centers. *Research in Nursing & Health, 22*, 15–25.

Hatzenbuehler, M. L., Schwab-Reese, L., Ranapurwala, S. I., Hertz, M. F., Marizen, R., & Ramirez, M. R. (2015). Associations between antibullying policies and bullying in 25 states. *Journal of American Medical Association Pediatrics, 169*(10); doi: 10.1001/jamapediatrics.2015.2411.

Hong, J. S. (2009). Feasibility of the Olweus bullying prevention program in low-income schools. *Journal of School Violence, 8*(1), 81–97.

Kärnä, A., Voeten, M., Little, T. D., Poskiparta, E., Alanen, E., & Salmivalli, C. (2011a). Going to scale: A nonrandomized nationwide trial of the KiVa antibullying program for grades 1–9. *Journal of Consulting and Clinical Psychology, 79*(6), 796–805.

Kärnä, A., Voeten, M., Little, T. D., Poskiparta, E., Kaljonen, A., & Salmivalli, C. (2011b). A large-scale evaluation of the KiVa antibullying program. *Child Development, 82*, 311–330.

Kärnä, A., Voeten, M., Little, T. D., Alanen, E., Poskiparta, E., & Salmivalli, C. (2013). Effectiveness of the KiVa antibullying program: Grades 1–3 and 7–9. *Journal of Educational Psychology, 105*(2), 535–551.

Lewis, K. M., DuBois, D. L., Bavarian, N., Acock, A., Silverthorn, N., Day, J., & Flay, B. R. (2013). Effects of positive action on the emotional health of urban youth: A cluster-randomized trial. *Journal of Adolescent Health.* doi:10.1016/j.jadohealth.2013.06.012

Limber, S. P. (2011). Development, evaluation, and future directions of the Olweus bullying prevention program. *Journal of School Violence, 10*, 71–87.

Limber, S. P., Nation, M., Tracy, A. J., Melton, G. B. & Flerx, V. (2004). Implementation of the Olweus bullying prevention program in the southeastern United States. In P. K. Smith, D. Pepler, & K. Rigby (Eds.), *Bullying in schools: How successful can interventions be?* (pp. 55–79). Cambridge, England: Cambridge University Press.

Lösel, F., & Beelmann, A. (2003). Effects of child skills training in preventing antisocial behavior: A systematic review of randomized evaluations. *Annals of the American Academy of Political and Social Science, 587*, 84–109.

McMahon, S. D., Wernsman, J., & Parnes, A. L. (2006). Understanding prosocial behavior: The impact of empathy and gender among African American adolescents. *Journal of Adolescent Health, 39*, 135–137.

Merrell, K. W., Isava, D., Gueldner, B. A., & Scott W. R. (2008). How effective are school bullying intervention programs? A meta-analysis of intervention research. *School Psychology Quarterly, 23*(1), 26–42.

Olweus, D. (1991). Bully/victim problem among school children: Basic facts and effects of a school-based intervention program. In D.J. Pepler & K.H. Rubin (Eds.), *The development and treatment of childhood aggression* (pp. 411–448). Hillsdale, NJ: Erlbaum.

Olweus, D. (1993). *Bullying at school. What we know and we can do.* Oxford, UK: Blackwell.

Olweus, D. (2001). Peer harassment: A critical analysis and some important issues. In J. Juvonen & S. Graham (Eds.), *Peer harassment in school: The plight of the vulnerable and victimized.* New York, NY: Guilford.

Olweus, D., & Limber, S. (2010). The Olweus bullying prevention program: Implementation and evaluation over two decades. In S. R. Jimerson, S. M. Swearer, & D. L. Espelage (Eds.), *The handbook of school bullying: An international perspective* (pp. 377–402). New York, NY: Routledge.

Salmivalli, C. Kaukiainen, A., & Voeten, M. (2005). Anti-bullying intervention: Implementation and outcome. British *Journal of Educational Psychology, 75*(2005), 465–487.

Smith P. K., Salmivalli, C., & Cowie, H. (2012). Effectiveness of school-based programs to reduce bullying: A commentary. *Journal of Experimental Criminology, 8,* 433–441.

Smith, J. D., Schneider, B. H., Smith, P. K., & Ananiadou, K. (2004). The effectiveness of whole-school antibullying programs: A synthesis of evaluation research. *School Psychology Review, 33*(4), 547–560.

Snyder, F. J., Flay, B. R., Vuchinich, S., Acock, A., Washburn, I. J., Beets, M. W., & Li, K.-K. (2010). Impact of a social-emotional and character education program on school level indicators of academic achievement, absenteeism, and disciplinary outcomes: A matched-pair, cluster randomized, controlled trial. *Journal of Research on Educational Effectiveness, 3*(1), 26–55.

Snyder, F. J., Vuchinich, S., Acock, A., Washburn, I. J., & Flay, B. R. (2012). Improving elementary school quality through the use of a social-emotional and character 14 development program: A matched-pair, cluster-randomized, controlled trial in Hawai'i. *Journal of School Health, 82*(1), 11–20. doi:10.1111/J.1746-1561.2011.00662.X

Swearer, S. M., Espelage, D. L., Vaillancourt, T., & Hymel, S. (2010). What can be done about school bullying? Linking research to educational practice. *Educational Researcher, 39,* 38–47. Retrieved from http://digitalcommons.unl.edu/edpsychpapers/141

Talbott, E., Celinska, D., Simpson, J., & Coe, M. C. (2002). Somebody else making somebody else fight: Aggression and the social context among urban adolescent girls. *Exceptionality, 10*(3), 203–220.

Ttofi, M., & Farrington, D. (2011). Effectiveness of school-based programs to reduce bullying: A systematic and meta-analytic review. *Journal of Experimental Criminology, 7*(2011), 27–56.

Veenstra, R., Lindenberg, S., Huitsing, G. Sainio, M., & Salmivalli, C. (2014). The role of teachers in bullying: The relation between antibullying attitudes, efficacy, and efforts to reduce bullying. *Journal of Educational Psychology, 106,* 1135–1143.

Washburn, I. J., Acock, A. C., Vuchinich, S., Snyder, F. J., Li, K.-K., Ji, P., & Flay, B. R. (2011). Effects of a social-emotional and character development program on the trajectory of behaviors associated with character development: Findings from three randomized trials. *Prevention Science, 12,* 314–323.

Yang, A., & Salmivalli, C. (2015). Effectiveness of the KiVa antibullying programme on bully-victims, bullies and victims. *Educational Research, 57*(1), 80–90.

Yeager, D. S., Fong, C. J., Lee, H. Y., & Espelage, D. L. (2015). Declines in efficacy of anti-bullying programs among older adolescents: A developmental theory and a three-level meta-analysis. *Journal of Applied Developmental Psychology, 37*(1), 36–51.

ENDNOTES

1   An experimental study is a type of evaluation that seeks to determine whether a program or intervention had the intended causal effect on program participants. There are three key components of an experimental study design: (1) *pre-post-test design*, (2) a *treatment group* and a *control group*, and (3) *random assignment* of study participants.

2   A quasi-experimental study is a type of evaluation that aims to determine whether a program or intervention has the intended effect on a study's participants. Quasi-experimental studies take on many forms but may best be defined as lacking key components of a true experiment. While a true experiment includes (1) pre-post-test design, (2) a treatment group and a control group, and (3) random assignment of study participants, quasi-experimental studies lack one or more of these design elements.

CHAPTER TEN

Restorative Justice in Schools

PRACTICING RESTORATIVE DISCIPLINE

J. Renee Trombley, Doshie Piper, and O. Oko Elechi

READING OBJECTIVES

- Discuss the concepts of restorative justice.
- Examine the intersection of schools and restorative justice.
- List and discuss several restorative principles, practices, and programs.
- Describe some specialty courts and juvenile probation and their roles in the implementation of restorative justice.

OVERVIEW

Restorative justice as a concept encapsulates a theory of justice that seeks to identify harm and engage all those who have been impacted by these events, in a process that allows for accountability, reparation, and restoration. Restorative justice processes attempt to engage all individuals who are considered key stakeholders, in a social justice process that is focused on restoring the harm that has been caused by crime, victimization, and injustice. Traditional models of restorative justice have been designed to focus on crime and restoration, and the key stakeholders in these events typically include the victim, the offender, and members of the surrounding community.

The emergence of restorative justice grew from disgruntled voices unhappy with the way justice was being handled in the American criminal justice system. Christie (1976) argued that the victim, the offender, their supporters and sympathizers, as well as the local community, were all the true owners of the conflict and not those professionals who were actually holding the power.

Those individuals include agents of law enforcement, those working in our courts including the prosecuting attorneys and judges, and those working in the corrections system and on parole boards. Yet, restorative justice emphasizes that the true stakeholders in these events are the ones who are directly affected by the crime or criminal behavior and that these individuals are those who will endure the aftermath of the conflict (victims, offenders, and community members), who most specifically deserve to play a part in the decision making process regarding how to seek justice for these cases.

The goals of restorative justice are realized through the identification of the harms caused by the act, identifying those responsible for such acts, and providing opportunities for accountability and restoration. This is very different from a traditional model of criminal justice which is focused on punishment and retribution. Instead of the justice process focusing on identifying offenders for punishment, the goals of a restorative justice process are healing the wounds caused by the act, seeking to restore the broken relationship, and making things as right as possible in the aftermath of harmful events, such as crime and criminal behavior.

Yet, it would be a misconception to believe that restorative justice is only about crime and criminal behavior. In fact, the concept of restorative justice, and the values and principles that underlie it, have led to the development of restorative processes in a multitude of ways, in a variety of spaces and places, and using both defined and undefined formats. In addition, this work occurs with various groups of people as well as being utilized in individually based processes. The development of restorative justice in the K-12 education system has been quite substantial over the last few decades and continues to grow as demand increases for more restorative approaches in dealing with student misbehavior and deviance. Also at the forefront of this growth are issues of harm and experiences with trauma among our student population, as well as a desire for more inclusive school environments focused on promoting social justice in our educational institutions.

RESTORATIVE JUSTICE CONCEPTS

One of the main concepts in restorative justice is healing through restoration. For many this means providing processes for addressing injustice, including after specific events of crime and criminal behavior. One focus for restorative justice is assisting victims in the process of restoration after suffering harm. Acknowledging that the victim suffered harm through physical violence or loss of property becomes necessary, and often victim vindication can be critical in promoting justice. Empowering victims and attending to their needs is very important. Efforts to restore the victim's dignity and sense of safety disparaged by the act must be made. And because victims are actively involved in the search for resolution to their pain and loss, they are more satisfied with the outcome. The second priority of the restorative justice process is to restore the community to the position it was in as much as possible. This is because restorative justice recognizes that the community is also a victim of crime. Understandably, when a member of the community suffers, the peace and well-being of the community is undermined. The community is a stakeholder and takes responsibility for the well-being of all community members, including the victim and the offender. The victim and the community are key to the justice process. The offenders are also stakeholders because, ideally, the restorative justice process must be inclusive and collaborative with decisions reached through a consensus. The third priority of restorative justice is to identify who is responsible for the harm caused by the act. The offender is held accountable for the act that harmed the victim and undermined the community's peace. Accountability does not equate to punishment. Rather, the offender must make right the harm he or she caused. It is also important to recognize the needs of the offender; true restorative justice options seek to restore all, including the offender, the victim, and the community. Ideally, transformation happens for all who are involved in the process and through this real restoration begins.

The offender is encouraged to show empathy and take full responsibility for the harm caused. Efforts are also made to address the needs and competencies of the offender that may be lacking. The offender has an obligation to restore the property or injury suffered by the victim. The offender must also acknowledge wrongdoing, show remorse, and make amends. According to Van Ness and Strong (2015), there are four elements to making amends. Amends, according to them, include apologizing for the acts that harmed others and paying restitution to the victims for their acts. They must also make efforts to change their behavior for the better and be generous. Generosity, in this case, means going beyond the demands of justice and equity to demonstrate remorse and responsibility to the victim, according to Van Ness and Strong (2015). Ideally, the offender's experience in the restorative justice process will lead to enhanced understanding and improved competency. Moreover, the victim and offender are more likely to have a sense of closure, which may lead to their reintegration into the community.

Restorative justice programs are capable of distinguishing between behaviors that are offensive and the individual responsible for that behavior. Braithwaite (1989) describes this approach to justice making as "reintegrative shaming." Offenders are treated respectfully as loved community members despite their vexing behavior. Community adjudicators are, therefore, able to send a message to the offender that their behavior is reprehensible but that their love for him or her remains intact if he or she can take steps to make amends. Punishment, according to this way of thinking, is not as effective in deterring people from offending as the people's fear of losing the love and respect of significant others in their lives.

DIFFERENCE IN APPROACH

Restorative justice, according to Zehr (2002, p.21), is principally different from the current criminal justice system. The following principles, according to Zehr, underpin the criminal justice system:

Criminal Justice System

1. What laws have been broken?
2. Who did it?
3. What does the person deserve?

On the other hand, restorative justice focuses on the following:

Restorative Justice

1. Who has been hurt?
2. What are their needs?
3. Whose obligations are these?

From this perspective, healing the victim and restoring peace to the community is the goal of justice rather than holding the law sacrosanct. We must not lose sight of the fact that laws are made to protect people and their property and to promote peace in the community. In the same vein, Pranis, Stuart, and Wedge (2003) observed that the emphasis of justice shifts from coercion to healing. Holding the offender accountable is not the same as punishing him or her. Punishing the offender may further alienate him or her and even polarize the community further. Furthermore, restorative justice seeks to repair the harm done while making efforts to prevent additional harm. Restorative justice recognizes that behaviors that result in harm may not necessarily be the responsibility of the offender alone.

The community must also take responsibility for the behavior of its members who harm others. Economic marginalization and our socialization institutions may be failing to meet society's desired goals. Oppressive economic and social infrastructure may be responsible for some deviant behaviors exhibited by community members. Pranis et al. (2003) insisted that justice processes must also shift from the goal of retribution to that of healing everybody, including victims, offenders, and the community. Conflict from the restorative justice perspective presents opportunities for the examination of the community's social and economic conditions that may partly be responsible for the conflict. Again, conflict presents opportunities for the teaching and relearning of the community's values and norms.

Restorative justice principles argue that justice must be transformative. In this regard, justice processes must seek to restore values and teachings that promote good behavior and community well-being. Our political, social, and economic policies as a society must promote human dignity and restore empathy. Economic and social justices are imperative to a healthy and progressive community. The justice process must restore participatory democracy (Elechi, 2006). The victims, offenders, and community members must be actively involved in defining harm and searching for a resolution that is healing and acceptable to all the stakeholders.

The value of respect, according to Zehr (2002), underlies the restorative justice process. Restorative justice teaches people to have respect for everyone, including those we do not share the same religion and culture with. Respect emphasizes our connectedness as human beings and overlooks the superficial differences that separate us. Without respect, we will not be able to reach a decision on any matter and that will polarize the community and make peace elusive.

SCHOOL POLICIES AND PRACTICES

The reality of zero-tolerance policies, high-stakes testing, and a culture of policing in schools, as well as the presence of disproportionate rates of school disciplinary procedures among students, overwhelmingly fuel the school-to-prison pipeline. This practice feeds into the carceral state in America while supporting and strengthening the prison industrial complex and ensuring the continuation of socially unjust practices and policies. Restorative justice has gained attention for the ability it has to provide a viable option for dismantling the school-to-prison pipeline, as well as addressing the harm that is created through ineffective practices in our educational institutions.

While originally envisioned as a response to harm within the justice system, a proliferation of restorative justice practices in the K–12 and higher education settings have taken place for over a decade now, and while not yet considered mainstream pedagogy, the growth of these practices is undeniable (Evans & Vaandering, 2016). In this section, we examine the goals and objectives of restorative justice in the K–12 education system and discuss specific strategies that educators and administrators use in the implementation of restorative justice policies and practices. In addition, restorative justice programs currently taking place in several schools are examined, and the overall effectiveness in reducing harm and providing alternatives to harsh disciplinary practices is also discussed.

In 2015, the U.S. DOE released a resource guide for administrators specifically aimed at improving school climate while addressing disciplinary issues that result in disproportionate numbers of minority students, as well as students with disabilities, being suspended or expelled at higher rates than their peers. The DOE reported data from the Civil Rights Data Collection, showing that African American youth are three times more likely than white students to be suspended or expelled, and together, Latino and African American youth make up more than 50% of those students referred to law enforcement or arrested for school-related offenses. In addition, the report noted that these disparities are evident even among our youngest children, with black students representing only 18% of students enrolled in preschool, yet they accounted for nearly half of all children who had been suspended more than once (U.S. DOE, 2015).

Policy Statement

These concerns were not new. In 2014, a letter issued by the U.S. Departments of Justice and Education, highlighting known disparities in disciplinary practices in our schools, especially among minority youth, was published, and a 2015 summit held at the White House concerned with these same issues took place. In response, the National Association of Community and Restorative Justice (NACRJ) released an official policy statement on restorative justice in K–12 education (NACRJ, 2017). Through this statement, the association recognized the need for suggested guidelines to support the implementation of restorative justice in schools specifically, and as such, called for the following:

1. All state education agencies to provide technical assistance to local school districts on the practice and implementation of "whole-school" restorative practices
2. Local education agencies, charter schools, and non-public schools to adopt school- or institution-wide climate practices to foster caring relationships and discipline policies that employ social engagement over social control
3. Institutions of higher education include the theory and practice of restorative justice in schools as part of teacher and school administrator licensure programs
4. Adults working with youth to adopt restorative practices for their own use, including building healthy relationships between each other, and have policies in place to repair the harm that may occur in conflicts between and among adults involved in educational systems

The policy statement provided by NACRJ offers 10 key elements representing a vision for school-wide restorative practices in K–12 education. According to their statement, the most important element requires the understanding that overall, relationships matter most, and this includes all members of the learning community, including faculty, staff, students, and the administration. Everyone is empowered through the whole-school approach to restorative justice in education, and power is shared through the use of inclusive practices and policy guidelines. Restorative justice recognizes that behavior can be seen as communication, and healing comes through reparation and support. Restorative schools provide education that is holistic while offering a curriculum that represents a multicultural and inclusive perspective. Finally, restorative schools are safe places built on the connectivity of relationships, and spaces where teachers truly believe in the potential of all of their students (NACRJ, 2017).

The DOE offers several key action items as strategies that superintendents can use as they seek to improve disciplinary procedures, school climate, and associated educational outcomes. These strategies involve the engagement of all stakeholders, including school board members, schoolteachers, staff members, students, and families, as well as members of the community. It is also important to establish clear goals, collect data and research to measure progress, and insist on transparency at all levels. In addition, it is important to provide ongoing support and training and to continue to review and revise policies and practices as needed (U.S. DOE, 2015). These strategies represent restorative approaches that can offer school-wide changes.

In 2016, researchers from Rutgers University, with the support of the Brooklyn Community Foundation, published a study on restorative justice implementation in four separate schools in Brooklyn and issued an executive summary based on their findings. They noted the importance of schools to develop a comprehensive vision for restorative practices when looking for transformative changes. This process involves recognizing the humanity of all the members of the school, valuing all of the voices that are represented, and providing opportunities to develop inclusiveness in classrooms and the school community. Administrators must assume responsibility for directing this paradigm shift and use an "all-in" approach to provide a foundation for a whole-school change, as well as provide opportunities for key stakeholders to engage in capacity-building practices that can promote long-term sustainability (Gregory, Soffer, Gaines, Hurley, & Karikehalli, 2016).

Schools can choose to support restorative justice initiatives in several ways through policies and practices. Many different options for achieving the goals of restorative justice in schools already exist. Restorative justice policies provide the foundation for a whole-school approach by seeking to reduce suspensions, expulsions, and other exclusionary disciplinary strategies instead of concentrating on reducing and restoring the harm created while focusing on relationships and communities in the process. Restorative justice practices support the application of these policies in schools and can be worked out through a variety of processes.

Restorative processes in schools can include peer mediation and peer juries, both focusing on including other students in the process. Peer mediations offer opportunities for learning conflict resolution skills, and peer juries can provide a meaningful way to involve students in discussions when rules and procedures in school are violated. Conferencing is another option and generally involves larger groups of people from the school community, including teachers, staff members, administrators, and students, as well as other key stakeholders such as family, friends, and community members. The common theme that these practices have is that they all involve a focus on reparation and restoration after a harm has been committed (Advancement Project, 2015; Pavelka, 2013).

Peacemaking circles are another form of restorative justice practice and offer numerous opportunities to support restoration and healing and to address specific needs within the school community and classrooms. Pranis (2005) provided an examination of several different types of circles, as well as practical applications that take place in schools. A wide variety of peacemaking circles can be used as needed and include purposes of talking, understanding, healing, sentencing, support, community building, conflict, reintegration, and celebration. These circles offer great potential for handling a variety of issues on school campuses and direct applications can include circles to support healing after traumatic incidents, sentencing circles that can provide alternatives to harsh school discipline, supporting circles for reintegration after suspension and expulsions, conferencing circles for academic support and development, peacemaking circles for building community and managing conflict, and celebration circles held throughout the school year for specific events (Pranis, 2005).

Circles are often used in classrooms to engage students in critical thought discussions, while giving value to each voice in the circle, and to build communities within the classroom. There is a large body of literature to support the implementation of restorative justice in schools and classrooms, not to mention a considerable number of videos online that can guide teachers to begin effectively engaging in these practices. Riestenberg (2012) offers a very useful publication for educators that provides a thorough description of restorative justice in the classroom, outlines processes for implementation of circles, and provides direct examples for how these processes can engage students.

Research in classrooms suggests that positive reinforcements work much better at improving school climate and discouraging disruptive behavior than punitive sanctions. Restorative processes in schools necessarily involve building trusting relationships; acknowledging values of peace, empathy, and respect among teachers, staff members, and students; and providing spaces and opportunities for engagement in these practices and processes. When actively facilitated within the classroom to enforce a culture of peacemaking, combined with a whole-school environment, these activities can effectively improve relationships and overwhelmingly reduce disruptive and deviant behavior (Smith, Fisher, & Frey, 2015).

Research has described outcomes associated with changing disciplinary procedures and improving school climates that include higher rates of attendance, high academic achievement, improving grades and test scores, strong attachment to school and peers, and enhanced relationships among students, teachers, and staff members. In addition, these practices work to decrease engagement in risky behaviors among students, including alcohol and drug use, and reduce the risk of violence while improving overall feelings of safety among students and staff (U.S. DOE, 2015).

These findings suggest the need for continuing to support the development and implementation of restorative justice practices and policies in educational settings. Yet there can be many challenges for those who wish to integrate restorative processes into their schools. Teachers are faced with the task of not only educating but also supporting, advising, inspiring, and disciplining students. These students often come with their own issues; many face challenges, and many more bring challenges to the classroom. In addition, current issues of school violence, low wages, and high testing demands can result in school cultures critical of peacemaking and restorative processes. Further recommendations to address these challenges include opportunities for professional development in restorative justice philosophy and practice for everyone in the school, including administrators, staff members, teachers, students, and even families. Schools must invest time, attention, and resources in developing the whole-school approach, and they should maintain a cohort of skilled restorative justice facilitators who use restorative processes at all levels, especially with disciplinary policies and strategies (Illinois Criminal Justice Information Authority, 2009).

Restorative justice offers a comprehensive and strategic opportunity to challenge and replace harsh disciplinary procedures, promote healing and restoration in schools, and build relationships while promoting peacemaking, as well as providing responsive justice when most needed. As schools embrace more holistic approaches in educational settings, progress can be made in dismantling the school-to-prison pipeline, reducing disproportionate graduation rates, addressing disproportionate rates of incarceration, and supporting the development of healthy and happy communities. This strategy just makes sense, and support should continue to develop at all levels of education legislation, including the national, state, and local levels. As a culture of violence in schools continues to dominate the media, peacemaking in schools offers an alternative, representing a paradigm shift that should be a priority. Through positive policies, programs, interactions, and relationships, true change is possible, along with all the hope for our future generations that it can bring.

JUVENILE JUSTICE IMPLICATIONS

Restorative justice outlines an alternative philosophy for addressing crime and delinquency. When students enter juvenile court processing, and thus the juvenile justice system, some new options need to be considered (Bazemore & Umbreit, 1994). First, it is important to consider who is making the decisions. Juvenile justice must change decision-making roles for juvenile offenders (students) who enter juvenile justice processing. Inclusive decision making on an appropriate set of obligations (or sanctions) by which juvenile offenders can satisfy restorative principles of accountability, competency development, and community safety aims within placement or processing can have a significant effect on changed behavior. This allows juvenile offenders to have a participatory role in the process (Bazemore & Umbreit, 1994).

Changing Decision-Making Roles

Direct participation by school administrators, teachers, or staff members and the juvenile offender in dispositional decisions through victim-offender dialogue is essential to addressing the harm between the institution and individual. This practice of participation can be useful to juvenile offenders in detention schools. Allowing youth to engage in dialogue while in detention schools can facilitate a clear educational path for students in confinement. According to Morris (2016), more than 70% of girls in confinement require trauma-informed care, and at least 60% have experienced rape or the threat of rape. Juvenile justice cannot ignore the impact of trauma. A restorative approach in which the juvenile offender is invited to share (dialogue) what is distracting him or her from an assignment and participation in the institutional education process that includes a member of the educational or institutional personnel responding with dignity creates a learning space where juvenile offenders are invited to engage critically alongside educators in the construction of their education and the redemption of their lives.

Direct participation by the victim (schools, school personnel, or other students), juvenile offender, and their respective communities of care (immediate or extended family, foster care or placement staff) in dispositional decisions through family group conferencing or similar community sanctioning and dispute resolution processes, including peacemaking sentencing, should be considered in juvenile justice processing (Bazemore & Umbreit, 1994). The result of a family group conference or a peacemaking sentencing approach would reshape the role of juvenile justice practitioners in the academic environment as agents of positive youth development (Butts, Jeffrey, Bazemore, & Meroe, 2010). The negotiation would recommend that the educators in the school detention facilities and the detention professionals collaborate, creating true partnerships designed to strategically or potentially help get juvenile offenders back into the traditional or community school and out of the institutional school (Schiff, 2013).

Many teachers who teach in juvenile detention facilities admit to feeling overwhelmed, unprepared, and insufficiently trained to deal with the numerous issues of the juvenile offenders they educate in juvenile hall. These restorative approaches "can help integrate and redefine the collaborative roles and relationships of educators and

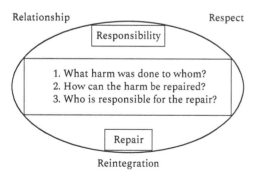

FIGURE 10.1 Restorative Language Creates a Context of Care

juvenile justice professionals by offering an inclusive and responsive structure for reengaging youth in the academic setting rather than further disenfranchising them from the school community" (Schiff, 2013).

Lastly, on changing decision-making roles by allowing juvenile offenders to directly participate in decision-making juvenile justice has to allow youth to be involved in the selection of community members in decisions through community panels. Let's examine Vermont's reparative boards.

Information from Vermont's Reparative Boards

Vermont was the first state to implement reparative boards in juvenile justice through probation conditions. In 1995, the State of Vermont decided to implement community justice processes that addressed the needs of the victims of crime, offenders who engaged in criminal behavior, and restored communities. The goal of these processes was to promote accountability and responsibility in offenders for their criminal behavior (Karp and Drakulich, 2004). Other researchers have also relied on Vermont's model. Boyes-Watson (2004) pointed out that it "is one of the earliest and most extensive statewide restorative initiatives in the United States" (p. 687). This alternative community reparative design was motivated by the increasing use of confinement in such a geographically small state. The community reparative model was not initially characterized as restorative but later gained recognition as a restorative practice (Perry & Gorczyk, 1997). It garnered its restorative designation because of its commitment to developing collaborative partnerships between criminal justice professionals, community members, and probationers (Comerford & Burford, 2002). The following is an example of how Vermont's reparative boards emerged:

> The emergence of reparative boards was consistent with other community-centered developments that were emerging in the state in the late 1980s and early 1990s in partnerships between the state government's Agency of Human Services—of which the Department of Corrections is a part—and local communities (Hogan, 1999; Mitchell, 2001; Perry, 1999). The program has enjoyed bipartisan and senior government support through transitions in governors, secretaries of the Agency of Human Services, and commissioners of the Department of Corrections. The somewhat unusual role of the Department of Corrections in spearheading the changes is noted as unique in the country. The use of volunteer community boards has been widely recognized as an innovative example of restorative justice and drawn considerable attention from researchers, policy makers, and public and community interest groups (Boyes-Watson, 2004; De Pommereau, 1997; Dooley, 1996; Goodenough, 1997; Immarigeon, 1997; Perry, 1997, Reno, 1997; Scott, 1996). In 1998, the Ford Foundation's Innovations in Government Award was awarded to the state in recognition of its work on reparative probation. Numerous board programs serving young offenders have been set up

across the United States using community boards (Schiff, Bazemore, & Erbe, 2001), and many of these cite Vermont's innovative program and leadership.

The reparative probation program provided that upon conviction of a minor, nonviolent crime, offenders may be sentenced to probation with the condition that they appear before a reparative board composed of trained citizen volunteers. The board, the offender, and the victim, should the person choose to attend, and other invited persons who have been affected by the crime meet and, when successful, negotiate an agreement in which the offender agrees to complete a number of tasks during the probationary period.

These agreements include tasks intended to help the offender better understand the harmful consequences of his or her behavior, repair the harm done to the victim, and restore the community to its pre-crime state. The agreements are intended to be developed around a strategy aimed at reducing reoffending.

(Excerpt from Humphrey, J. A., Burford, G., & Huey, M. P. (2006). *Reparative versus standard probation: Community justice outcomes* (Grant No. 2000IJCX0033). Washington, DC: U.S. Department of Justice.)

This reparative approach would allow juvenile offenders the opportunity to remain in their community schools and not force them to learn in lockdown. A restorative function of reparative boards would be to aid schools in reengaging youth at risk of academic failure and juvenile justice system entry by creating agreements regarding misbehavior that help keep youth in school, off the streets, and out of detention.

Moving Toward Restorative Justice in Teen Courts

How restorative teen court principles are implemented will vary based on local resources, traditions, and cultures. All teen court program models (i.e., adult judge, youth judge, youth tribunal, and peer jury) have the potential to incorporate restorative justice–based practices if staff members and program organizers are flexible and open to new ideas related to program policies, procedures, and practices. Leadership from judges and prosecutors in facilitating restorative alternatives to the traditional court system is essential in teen court program models. Teen courts can serve as a mechanism to assist low-level juvenile offenders in their communities and schools and out of juvenile detention.

It is important to consider the true victims of school misbehavior and disciplinary infractions, such as assault and violent or potentially violent behavior, and gain community input through victim and community impact statements to the juvenile court. Teen courts appear to be moving toward restorative justice–based practices as an ongoing process that seems appropriate for hearing victim and community impact statements (Godwin, 2001). There is no single "right way" to implement the restorative justice concept in teen courts. One possibility for the juvenile justice system to address victims and communities indirectly is through seeking their input through client satisfaction surveys administered by juvenile court professionals. Another way to invite victims' input is by including victims' representatives in the teen court process.

It is safe to say that no teen court is fully restorative in nature and may never be because of some of the practices and philosophies that define a teen court (Godwin, 2001). However, programs can definitely be more restorative than they are currently. Change is slow and a learning process. Program staff and organizers who decide to move toward more restorative justice–based practices will need to assess and reassess where they are in the application of restorative justice principles constantly and adjust practices accordingly. While it may be easier to implement restorative justice concepts as a program is being developed, there are ways to build on the strengths of an existing teen court program to make it more restorative.

Juvenile Justice Professionals Engaging the Community

In Chapter 6, probation was discussed as a post-arrest proceeding. Keeping with the implementation of restorative justice in juvenile courts, professional role changes need to take place. The following promising practice reflects how changing the roles of juvenile justice professionals worked in a balanced and restorative justice practice and resulted in greater community involvement, support, and ownership. Let's examine Minnesota.

> In Minnesota, a probation officer became frustrated with the failure of available interventions to change the behavior patterns of juvenile offenders from a particular school. Juvenile offenders were in and out of the system repeatedly, both on new offenses and on violations of conditions of probation or supervised release. Looking for a solution, the officer began discussions with a social service provider who suggested a vocational educational program. (Bazemore & Umbreit, 1994)

Restorative justice planning allowed the probation officer (juvenile justice professional) and social service provider the flexibility to explore restorative justice options. The juvenile justice professional obtained written material on various restorative justice program models from the restorative justice planner at the Minnesota Youth Corrections Department. Then he shared and discussed the restorative justice material with a juvenile court judge and prosecutor. Having engaged the judge's interest, the juvenile justice professional identified key leaders in the target community, school, and justice system. In conjunction with the social service provider, the juvenile justice professional organized a seminar to introduce restorative justice and possible program models to the group. The juvenile justice professional recruited speakers, sent invitations, made personal contacts to encourage attendance, and facilitated the meeting to implement restorative practices in Minnesota.

SUMMARY

Restorative justice offers an effective alternative to traditional punishment. Restorative justice is a process that provides opportunities for communities, offenders, and victims to engage in dialogue aimed at reducing harm while providing opportunities for healing among victims and developing accountability in offenders. Restorative justice programs and practices seek to build transformative conversations, policies, and practices. This breaks with the current criminal justice system agenda but finds hope brewing among many advocates. In particular, restorative justice has found support in the criminal and juvenile justice systems and is more extensively discussed in the field of K–12 education.

Restorative justice is slowly building a home in the field of education, both in the K–12 education system and on college and university campuses across the United States. There are a number of ways that restorative justice is emerging, mostly through a ground-up approach, and it includes changes to the whole-school environment using the values and philosophies of restoration through practices, programs, and policies, as well as more minimal approaches at the classroom level. Overall, there continues to be support for the ability of these processes to support a healthy and healing classroom and school experience. In addition, these policies and practices can reduce disparities in school disciplinary procedures and offer an opportunity to divert youth from the school-to-prison pipeline.

Nowhere is restorative justice needed more than in the structure of the juvenile justice system, and research shows that current attempts at integrating restorative programming are proving successful on a variety of measures. Youth engaged in these practices show reduced rates of recidivism and higher levels of accountability through involvement with community service and restitution completion. Finally, it is important to consider the impact that is reported by everyone involved in these processes, including offenders, victims, community members, family members, teachers, and practitioners. Overwhelmingly, the tales from the field suggest positive and encouraging support for restorative justice as a whole.

DISCUSSION QUESTIONS

1. Who are the stakeholders in a restorative justice process? Whose needs should be considered?
2. How can administrators support restorative justice in schools?
3. Describe the use of peacemaking circles and ways that they can be implemented in schools.

4. How might a juvenile probation officer use restorative justice processes in his or her work?
5. How might teen courts respond to incidents of misconduct in schools?

REFERENCES

Advancement Project (2014). *Restorative practices: Fostering healthy relationships & promoting positive discipline in schools*. Retrieved from https://advancementproject.org/resources/restorative-practices-fostering-healthy-relationships-promoting-positive-discipline-in-schools/

Bazemore, G., & Umbreit, M. (1994). *Balanced and restorative justice*. Washington, DC: U.S. Department of Justice, Office of Juvenile Justice and Delinquency Prevention.

Boyes-Watson, C. (2004). The value of citizen participation in restorative/community justice: Lessons from Vermont. *Criminology and Public Policy, 3*, 687–692.

Braithwaite, J. (1989). *Crime, shame and reintegration*. New York, NY: Cambridge University Press.

Butts, Jeffrey A., Bazemore, G., & Meroe, A. S. (2010). *Positive youth justice-framing justice interventions using the concepts of positive youth development*. Washington, DC: Coalition for Juvenile Justice.

Christie, N. (1976). *Conflict as property* (no. 23). Oslo, Norway: Institute for Criminology and Criminal Law Stencil Series.

Comerford, S., & Burford, G. (2002). *Community by community: Strengthening Vermont's youth justice system through collaboration*. Burlington, VT: University of Vermont, Department of Social Work.

De Pommereau, I. (1997, Summer). In the heart of a community. *Vermont Life*, 60–63.

Dooley, M., (1996). Restorative justice in Vermont: A work in progress. In E. Barajas (Ed.), *Community justice: Striving for safe, secure, and just communities* (pp. 31–36). Washington, DC: National Institute of Corrections.

Elechi, O. O. (2006). *Doing justice without the state: The Afikpo (Ehugbo) Nigeria model*. New York, NY: Routledge.

Evans, K., & Vaandering, D. (2016). *The little book of restorative justice in education: Fostering responsibility, healing, and hope in schools*. New York, NY: Good Books Publishing.

Godwin, T. (2001). *The role of restorative justice in teen courts: A preliminary look*. Lexington, KY: National Youth Court Center.

Goodenough, O. (1997). Biology, behavior, and criminal law. *Vermont Law School, 4*.

Gregory, A, Soffer, R., Gaines, E., Hurley, A., & Karikehalli, N. (2016). *Implementing Restorative Justice in Schools: Lessons Learned from Restorative Justice Practitioners on Four Brooklyn Schools*. Brooklyn, NY: Brroklyn Community Foundation.

Hogan, C. (1999). *Vermont communities count: Using results to strengthen services for families and children.* The Annie E. Casey Foundation. Retrieved from http://www.aecf.org/publications/vermont.pdf

Humphrey, J. A., Burford, G., & Huey, M. P. (2006). *Reparative versus standard probation: Community justice outcomes* (Grant No. 2000IJCX0033). Washington, DC: U.S. Department of Justice.

Illinois Criminal Justice Information Authority. (2009). *Implementing restorative justice—victims, offender, community: A guide for schools.* Chicago, IL : Illinois Criminal Justice Information Authority. Retrieved from http://www.icjia.state.il.us/publications/implementing-restorative-justice-a-guide-for-schools

Immarigeon, R. (1997). Probation and domestic violence: New parameters, model practices. *Community Corrections Report on Law and Corrections Practice, 4*(6), 91–94.

Karp, D. R., & Drakulich, K. M. (2004). Minor crime in a quaint setting: Practices, outcomes, and limits of Vermont reparative probation boards. *Criminology & Public Policy, 3*(4), 655–686.

Mitchell, C. (2001). *Outcome-based planning: State partner and local communities working together to improve the well-being of all Vermonters.* State Team for Children, Families and Individuals. Waterbury, VT: State of Vermont, Agency of Human Services.

Morris, M. (2016). *Pushout: The criminalization of black girls in schools.* New York, NY: The New Press.

National Association of Community and Restorative Justice (NACRJ). (2017). *NACRJ policy statement of restorative justice in K–12 education.*

Pavelka, S. (2013). Practices and policies for implementing restorative justice within schools. *The Prevention Researcher, 20*(1), 15–17.

Perry, J. (1997). Reciprocity, and criminal justice using epigenetics rules to design a program. *Vermont Law Review, 22,* 407–423.

Perry, J. G., & Gorczyk, J. F. (1997). Restructuring corrections: Using market research in Vermont. *Corrections Management Quarterly, 1,* 26–35.

Pranis, K. (2005) *The little book of circle processes: A new/old approach to peacemaking.* New York, NY: Good Books Publishing.

Pranis, K., Stuart, B. & Wedge, M. (2003). *Peacemaking circles: From crime to community.* St. Paul, Minnesota: Living Justice Press.

Riestenberg, N. (2012). *Circle in the square: Building community and repairing harm in school.* St. Paul, Minnesota: Living Justice Press.

Reno, J. (1997). Regaining public confidence. *State Government News,* 16–19.

Schiff, M. (2013, January). *Dignity, disparity, and desistance: Effective restorative justice strategies to plug the "school-to-prison pipeline."* Paper presented at the Center for Civil Rights Remedies National Conference, Closing the School to Research Gap: Research to Remedies, Washington, DC.

Schiff, M., Bazemore, G., & Erbe, C. (2001). *Tracking restorative justice decision making in the response to youth crime.* The Prevalence of Youth Conferencing in the United States. The Community Justice Institute, Florida Atlantic University, Ft. Lauderdale.

Smith, D., Fisher, D., & Frey, N. (2015). *Better than carrots or sticks.* Alexandria, VA: ASCD

U.S. Department of Education. (U.S. DOE). (2015). *Rethink school discipline: School district leader summit on improving school climate and discipline, resource guide for superintendent action.* Retrieved from https://www2.ed.gov/policy/gen/guid/school-discipline/rethink-discipline-resource-guide-supt action.pdf

Van Ness, D. W. & Strong, K. H. (2015). *Restoring justice- An introduction to restorative justice.* New York: NY: Routledge.

Zehr (2002). *The little book of restorative justice.* New York, NY: Good Books Publishing.

Figure Credit

Fig. 10.1: Source: https://www.resolutionariesinc.com/wp-content/uploads/2014/05/Screen-Shot-2014-05-07-at-3.10.00-PM.png.

CHAPTER ELEVEN

Evaluation of School-Based Programs

Katalin Parti

READING OBJECTIVES

- Understand the necessity of an evaluative assessment and the documentation of a school-based anti-bullying program.
- Identify the internal and external validity problems that can influence program effects.
- Explain the reasons why an anti-bullying program proven to be successful in the original set of circumstances might fail to bring the same positive results in another setting.
- List the ways in which the phenomenon of bullying can best be assessed.

OVERVIEW

Can we say that a school violence program is successful if the data does not justify it? And is a program necessarily and exclusively unsuccessful if no apparent change takes place in its footsteps? It may be surprising, but yes might be the answer to both questions.

There are factors in the environment, in the composition of the population, in history, in the measurement tool, in the timing of the measurement, in the interaction of the participating groups, or in the person of the program leader, which can influence the results of the measurement separately and together. It is important to know these potential influencing factors, as we can argue with them about the success of the program or against the continuation of the program, despite its seemingly good results.

This chapter gives guidance on what circumstances need to be kept in mind to be able to (1) select the results taking place in a program *regardless*, or *in spite of*, the particular program and to be able to (2) identify the real effects of a given program by eliminating program-independent factors. Referring to the anti-bullying programs described in detail in Chapter 9, this chapter explains why it is important for schools to document their school violence programs properly. Finally, it elaborates a proposal for the program's documentation, which allows for the separation of the effects and thus the repetition of the program.

EVALUATIVE ASSESSMENT PROBLEMS

Program effect can be approached from the aspect of **internal validity** and **external validity**. During an evaluation, internal validity is an indicator of the extent to which the measured or identified change is caused by the stimulus used—in our case anti-bullying programs. External validity is the extent to which results can be generalized (i.e., an indicator of the extent to which the characteristics of the sample population correspond to the characteristics of the total population). In anti-bullying programs, this indicates the extent to which the school in the sample shows the same characteristics as all schools or the targeted age groups.

Internal Validity Problems
A distortion of **internal validity** may have several causes (Enders, 2010; Langbeim, 2006, pp. 57–75; Shadish, Cook, & Campbell, 2002).

History Effect or External Events Effect
The Olweus program was introduced into schools on a national scale in the wake of several highly publicized suicides that were linked to bullying (Olweus, 1993). It seems likely that as a result, there was a lot of pressure on Norwegian schools, as they were expected to take immediate and spectacular steps to prevent bullying. This is called "history effect" or "external events effect." It is also possible that the program suddenly brought such good results because it had the power of novelty. This is confirmed by the Second Step study, where the evaluation only produced results in the first year (Espelage, Low, Polanin, & Brown, 2013; Frey, Nolen, Van Schoiack-Edstrom, & Hirschstein, 2005). Logically, the development in such cases is not only because of the program but also because *society becomes more sensitized toward bullying because of external events.*

Norm loss may be caused by the frequent change in authority (school management) or frequent change in prevention programs (and within that inconsistency—i.e., the frequent change in drives, goals, and motivation triggers). Such a system change has been observed in a wider societal context. It involves changes in norms and the legislative environment as a result of which the constant change in regulations leads to legal uncertainty and loss of norms (Durkheim, 1951 [1897]; Merton, 1938). A good example is a school where frequent changes in management, staff, rules, or even violence programs may cause uncertainty in students and devaluation of the constantly changing rules.

Differences were found in the test of the Second Step middle school program between schools in Kansas and Illinois, despite the fact that they used a matched pair random control trial, which means that the main characteristics were homogeneous across the schools and classes. Espelage explained the weaker performance of schools in Kansas by citing that turnover was higher in administrative staff, which made the school atmosphere unfavorable for the program (Espelage, Low, Polanin, & Brown, 2015). Turnover may have had an influence on the results of an earlier evaluation of Second Step in New England as well: school administrators had to evaluate (on a grading scale) the antisocial behavior of students on three different occasions. However, because of the changes in staff, children might have had more than one assessor, which disrupted consistency and made the evaluation unreliable (Taub, 2001).

The history effect can be decreased in longitudinal programs based on the age-cohort design because the program effects are to be investigated in many different time periods, which provides high validity (Olweus, 2005).

Testing Effect
The history effect is comparable to the testing effect, as sensitivity grows in both cases because of current events. There are cases in which even the control group shows positive changes. It is possible that the control and intervention groups are not properly separated (they come from the same school), so they *contaminate* each other's results (Parti, Schmidt, & Néray, 2018). It is also possible that a baseline survey has such a sensitizing effect that the indices of the control group improves (Olweus, 2005).

Maturation, Trend, Endogenous Change
Ttofi and Farrington's meta-analysis (2011) showed that school violence programs were most effective in middle schools or above that. Smith and his colleagues, nonetheless, believe that it is the younger age groups that have the flexibility and can, therefore, be influenced positively (Smith et al., 2012). It is also likely that the precise rules that adults represent are not easily followed later in the children's teens because of their growing independence. For younger children, adults have a leading and protective status, and the students easily obey their instructions (Salmivalli et al., 2005). If, therefore, the program effect is reduced as teenagers mature, then this may be interpreted as a result of their growing autonomy, independent of the program.

The control group can be used to control the effect of developmental changes. Very often, the program has no other positive effect other than achieving a stagnation in the prevalence of bullying with progressing age. Although the prevalence of bullying shows a rise with age, it, nevertheless, can be said that a positive change occurred in the treatment. This change can be tracked by applying a control group. Similar observations were made during the evaluation of Steps to Respect: Although the physical bullying perpetration scale score increased from pre- to posttest in both the intervention and control schools, the increase was smaller in the intervention schools (Brown, Low, Smith, & Haggerty, 2011).

Instrumentation

Research projects very often take a single data type into consideration when assessing program effectiveness. For example, the Second Step middle school program's results were measured only in one way, with the observational questionnaires of independent observers. Self-report measures that supported the results were missing, which caused a monoinformant bias (Espelage et al., 2013). To increase the reliability of evaluations, the triangular method is recommended. This means using more resources or methods (e.g., student questionnaires, teacher questionnaires, teacher observations, parent reports) to measure the same phenomenon. The multi-informant approach is expressly preferred to measure school bullying (Ladd & Kochenderfer-Ladd, 2002). It is argued that in the area of bullying research, it is typical that the status designations of bully, victim, bully victim, and bystander are based on one informant, mostly the child. This, however, increases the possibility of measurement errors. When measuring prevalence, not only the opinion of the children but also those of the teachers need to be surveyed, for example, by using teacher rating scales. In school-based prevention programs, parents prove to be the least accessible group; in the Positive Action program, for example, they had to stop implementing family surveys (Positive Action Evaluation Report, 2014, p. 36). In such cases, researchers usually compare the results of the self-report tests of students with the observation-based responses of another adult group (e.g., teachers).

Regression Threat

Probability sampling and random assignment of schools are both tools for increasing the reliability of samples. Applying either of these, schools will have the same likelihood of being selected either into the intervention group or into the control group. This makes generalization possible, which means that the schools participating in the survey can be representative (or a mirror) of the characteristics of all schools in the district. However, random assignment to treatment and control conditions is difficult to implement in anti-bullying programs, as it is usually the more motivated schools that anticipate more activity, so these are the ones selected into the treatment group rather than into the control (Smith, Schneider, Smith, & Ananiadou, 2004). In parallel, the dropout rate of the control group is higher, which also reduces the validity of the results. In the Positive Action program, for example, the participating schools were heterogeneous in terms of race, ethnic, and socioeconomic background. Even though an agreement was reached with schools before the implementation of the program that they selected randomly into the treatment or control group, more motivated schools would rather have chosen the treatment group, while less motivated ones would have chosen the control group. To keep high validity, only those schools that adhered to the randomized matched sampling criterion were kept in the sample. The program lost a large number of schools this way (Bavarian et al., 2013; Beets et al., 2009; Lewis et al., 2013; Li et al., 2011). A cross-section of urban and rural areas in the sample may also contribute to higher validity (Smith & Shu, 2000).

Attrition or Experimental Mortality
Attrition or experimental mortality may significantly distort research results (Farrington, 2003; Olweus, 1991; Washburn et al., 2011). The reason for this might be that (1) they target several different groups of people at the same time (e.g., students from different grades or students and adults, or adults of a different status—e.g., educators and parents), (2) the assessed population is heterogeneous in many ways (e.g., students of low-income urban schools and students of high-income private schools (Lewis et al., 2013), (3) the turnover of the sample population is very fast (Lewis et al., 2013), or (4) attrition is more likely if the program is assessing a very large sample, such as a whole community (school, parents, residential community, prison, boarding institutions, etc.). In such programs, the initial enthusiasm needs to be maintained for long years to achieve fidelity, and constant activity of participants is needed to have any real effect on the school atmosphere and to achieve the promised preventive effect. In economically and socially disadvantaged communities, however, where this effect would be needed the most (e.g., among ethnic minorities, communities below the poverty line, regions with high unemployment or criminality, negatively discriminated social groups, subcultures), it takes an even bigger effort to achieve changes. Consequently, a longer time and more motivation are needed for participation. Program leaders can motivate control schools with financial benefits or the offer of a delayed introduction of the treatment.

Some schools stop antiviolence programs after 2–3 years because they have worked. The incident rate becomes low, so the school administration believes there is no need to continue with the program. But some of these schools have found that it only takes another 2 to 3 years for problem behaviors to return to the previous levels, as incoming students who never received any sensitization begin to influence the student body (Li et al., 2011). A 3- to 4-year longitudinal follow-up study might show larger effect sizes (Frey, Hirschstein, Edstrom, & Snell, 2009).

In (longitudinal) school violence programs, attrition-due data distortion can be best avoided by using the **age-cohort design** sampling method. Strictly speaking, age-cohort design cannot be regarded as a longitudinal survey, as it does not measure the characteristics of the same group every year but rather the development seen in the consecutive age cohorts (Olweus, 2005). The method was used first by Olweus in Norway to test the Olweus Bullying Prevention Program, where children of a certain age in year 1 before the intervention were compared with different children of the same age in the same school after the intervention in year 2 (Olweus, 1991).

Multiple Treatment Interference

The effect of a program is practically impossible to measure if other anti-bullying programs are also in use at the same time, causing multiple treatment interference. It is not possible to neutralize the effects of other programs, even if the subject of the parallel program is not, or not expressly, anti-bullying sensitization. There is also no guarantee that the achieved positive effect was exclusive because of the given program component. It is possible that several components or parallel programs had a combined effect, which manifests as a drop in perpetration and the victimization index.

It is also possible that parallel programs are actually weakening each other. One possible reason for this is that several prevention programs (and curricula) are running at the schools at the same time, and students have lost interest (Frey et al., 2005). This sends the message for program developers, school principals, and guidance counselors that care must be taken to make the curriculum particularly interesting, diverse, and attractive, and that it should be constantly updated and follow students' needs (Espelage et al., 2015).

External Validity Problems

External validity may be threatened by the effect of factors occurring independently of the treatment. Such is, for example, the cultural effect (the program will have a different effect in different cultures), the socioeconomic effect (a heterogeneous economic environment will affect external validity), the instrument of measure (if another instrument is used in the survey, it will distort results), the person performing the measuring (the program effect is influenced by the personal effect of those participating in implementation), or the documentation effect (the program is not sufficiently described for others to replicate) (Bracht & Glass, 1968; Gall, Borg, & Gall, 1996). Problems related to internal and external validity are closely linked, and their effects cannot really be separated.

Population Heterogeneity

The most crucial problem that might occur in relation to external validity has to do with population heterogeneity. No matter how well a program worked on the European continent, because of the heterogeneity of cultural, school system, ethnic, economic, and socioeconomic indices, it cannot be adapted in the United States without modification. Despite the fact that gross domestic product per capita is relatively high in the United States, the differences between the highest and lowest layers of society are bigger than in Scandinavia and Western Europe, and relative poverty is also higher (Evans, Frazer, & Cotter, 2014; Iceland, 2006). Poverty shows a correlation with behavioral problems in childhood, early school leaving, post-traumatic stress disorder, depression, criminal behavior, and a low rate of participation in education. Anti-bullying programs developed in Europe or elsewhere cannot cope with these challenges. Research has not yet confirmed which are the factors of homogeneity or which cause low performance in students. Schools in poorer communities often have higher rates of both teacher and student turnover, as well as lower levels of teacher experience and training. Schools with economically poor and diverse student populations have lower academic scores, lower attendance rates, higher truancy, and less parent involvement. Students often face elevated stress, depression, and diminished emotion regulation capacities (Hess & Copeland, 2001), so it is difficult to engage them in classroom work. Therefore, the effects of the single components need to be assessed separately, and the programs need to be modified in line with the needs assessment.

THE FIVE DS OF EVALUATION: DESIGN, DOCUMENTATION, DISCOVERY, DURATION, AND DEVELOPMENT

A proper program evaluation has five prerequisites: design, documentation, discovery, duration, and development (Figure 11.1).

Design
You must design your study well before you actually launch your program. We have seen the importance of the preparation of the program not only from a content but also a methodology point of view. The preparation includes developing supporting materials to make the work of the targeted group easier during implementation (i.e., guidelines, policy-making guides, and form templates). The number of people who should be involved in the implementation has to be elaborated, as well as what qualities, education, professional experience, personality traits, and human capital these people should have for the programs to be implemented properly. Intervention studies that use solid experimental or quasi-experimental design and measure the effects of actual bullying behaviors, as well as perceptions and knowledge, are strongly recommended.

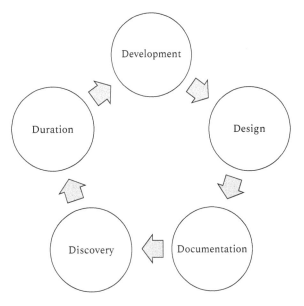

FIGURE 11.1   The Five Ds of evaluation rules: Design, Documentation, Discovery, Duration, and Development
Source: K. Parti.

Documentation
The preparation of the program, sampling, the first contact with schools, and implementation all need

to be documented. Documenting the problems related to evaluation, shortcomings, and difficulties identified along the way is important for the reliability (replicability) and validity (suitability for the assessment of the given phenomenon) of the research. Implementation procedures should be transparent to allow researchers to observe whether effects are related to the key features of the intervention or the key features of the evaluation. The better documented a program is, the more credible it will be. This also increases the dedication of schools and the motivation of participating educators, which also helps improve the degree of implementation and in the end guarantees the success of the program.

Documenting unexpected, neutral, or even negative results is not only important for the transparency of the program but also encourages the development of good practices in other schools. Also, documenting the development history of programs may provide lessons not only for the program schools but also for the evolution of programs aimed at similar issues.

Discovery

It is very important to review the findings of other programs when defining the assessment criteria. In addition, the assessment of new phenomena should be included in the research that has evaded the attention of earlier researchers. We should strive to forecast the trends of changing phenomena. Notorious perpetrators, the phenomena underlying the behavior of popular children and bystanders, or the assessment of group dynamics are, for example, novelties in anti-bullying programs. Programs should be built up using a strict methodology, with the principles of reliability and validity in mind. This is what makes our research reproducible and comparable to the findings of other well-documented and methodologically sound research.

Duration

Duration refers to the time frame of longitudinal programs, the data surveys repeated at consistent intervals and with consistent settings, and the systematic monitoring of the programs. Only a longitudinal study can show whether the assessed program fulfills the hopes for its success, while at the same time, longitudinal design is a prerequisite of anti-bullying prevention and intervention (e.g., age-cohort design, quasi-experimental design). The annual data survey has to be conducted at the same time every year, under standard conditions (e.g., online questionnaire in class settings, without the homeroom teacher's presence but with the presence of the project control person). Duration also applies to the continuous monitoring of participating schools in the interest of maintaining dedication, motivation, and competence.

Development

Finally, problems solved during evaluation, the solutions found, and, in general, all evaluation experience should be incorporated into the program. Policy and practice implications need to be formulated, and the evaluation outcomes are to be summarized in a format suitable for use by practical experts and policy makers. This is worth doing even if it demands more time, as the main output of prevention and intervention programs is their applicability in practice.

JUVENILE JUSTICE IMPLICATIONS

By documenting the anti-bullying programs' steps properly, the school administration produces evidence of its efforts to make the school environment safe. By applying a methodologically correct evaluation, schools provide evidence that the anti-bullying effort they made contributed to the safer school environment. In connection to that, program failures can be eliminated in the future.

In Chapter 7 (concerning pertinent legal cases), we saw that jurisdictions often favor a school administration's interests over students' rights. However, when the school's interest (to keep the school environment safe) and the students' rights (for free speech, etc.) clash, and the students file suit against the school that has violated their fundamental rights, the school might be able to provide evidence that it took proactive steps for maintaining and assessing a safe school environment.

In the case of *Wisniewski v. Board of Education of the Weedsport Central School District* (2007) (United States Court of Appeals, Second Circuit, Docket No. 06-3394-cv.) discussed in detail in Chapter 7, Aaron Wisniewski used an icon on an instant messenger site to identify himself that he asserted toward his 15 friends on his "buddy list" that contained an offensive message: "Kill Mr. VanderMolen," his English teacher. The superintendent decided that the icon was threatening and disrupted the school environment. Therefore, Aaron was charged under the New York Education Law for violation of school rules and suspended for a semester as a consequence. A year later, his parents filed suit against the board of education and the superintendent. One count claimed that the board and the superintendent had failed to train the school staff on threat assessment, and the lack of such training and a missing protocol to deal with similar cases led to the violation of the First Amendment rights of the child.

Therefore, the best way to prove that proactive measures are provided to strengthen a safe school environment is to keep record of the anti-bullying program efforts, make clear rules of dos and don'ts on-campus and off-campus, display protocols of how the institution handles wrongdoings and misdemeanors, and make these processes transparent. To achieve these foregoing requirements, the aforementioned rules of documentation should be respectfully followed.

SUMMARY

This chapter showed that the distortion of internal validity may have several reasons. Among them are history (or external events) effect, such as societal changes; turnover in school management; and frequent change in prevention programs. Internal validity can be threatened by testing effects, maturation, instrumentation, regression threat, attrition (or experimental mortality), and multiple treatment interference.

However, the external validity of a school-based program may be threatened by factors independent of the treatment, such as the cultural effect and population heterogeneity. We have seen evidence that no matter how well a program worked on the premises of its origin, because of the heterogeneity of the cultural patterns, the school system, and the ethnic, economic, and socioeconomic indices, the program cannot be introduced elsewhere without modification.

When planning anti-bullying programs, we need to take into consideration some important lessons learned from the methodology literature and confirmed by anti-bullying programs:

- Longitudinal programs can diminish history effect.
- A 3- or 4-year longitudinal follow-up study might show larger effect sizes.
- Control groups have to be applied to control the effect of the program. Control schools need to match the program schools in the sample.
- Probability sampling and random assignment of schools are tools for increasing sample reliability.
- It is recommended that researchers use various evaluative methods (triangularity) to measure the same phenomenon.
- Research design methods, such as age-cohort design sampling, can help avoid attrition-due data distortion.
- Possible barriers of implementation need to be investigated before adapting any program in a foreign country.
- A proper and thorough program evaluation is needed to ensure validity and replicability of the program.

DISCUSSION QUESTIONS

1. Identify the internal and external validity problems that can influence program effect.
2. Explain the reasons why an anti-bullying program proven to be successful in the original set of circumstances might fail to bring the same positive results in another setting.

3. What are the elements of a proper program evaluation? List some reasons why an evaluative assessment is needed to test program effect.
4. Bring up arguments as to why thorough program documentation is needed to ensure validity and replicability.

REFERENCES

Bavarian, N., Lewis, K. M., DuBois, D. L., Acock, A., Vuchinich, S., Silverthorn, N., ... & Flay, B.R. (2013). Using social-emotional and character development to improve academic 11 outcomes: A matched-pair, cluster-randomized controlled trial in low-income, urban schools. *Journal of School Health, 83*(11), 771–779.

Beets, M. W., Flay, B. R., Vuchinich, S., Snyder, F. J., Acock, A., Li, K. K. & Durlak, J. A. (2009). Use of a social and character development program to prevent substance use, violent behaviors, and sexual activity among elementary students in Hawaii. *American Journal of Public Health, 99*(8), 1438–1445.

Bracht, G. H., & Glass, G. V. (1968). The external validity of experiments. *American Education Research Journal, 5*, 437–474.

Brown, E.C., Low, S., Smith, B. H., & Haggerty, K. P. (2011). Outcomes from a school-randomized controlled trial of Steps to Respect: A bullying prevention program. *School Psychology Review, 40*(3), 423–443.

Durkheim, E. (1951) [1897]. *Suicide: A study in sociology.* New York: NY: The Free Press.

Enders, C. K. (2010). *Applied missing data analyses.* New York, NY: Guilford.

Espelage, D. L., Low, S., Polanin, J. R., & Brown, E. (2013). The impact of middle school program to reduce aggression, victimization, and sexual violence. *Journal of Adolescent Health, 53*(2), 180–186.

Espelage, D. L., Low, S., Polanin, J. R. & Brown, E. C. (2015). Clinical trial of Second Step© middle-school program: Impact on aggression and victimization. *Journal of Applied Developmental Psychology, 37*(1), 52—63, https://doi.org/10.1016/j.appdev.2014.11.007

Evans, C.B.R., Frazer, M. W., & Cotter, K. L. (2014). The effectiveness of school-based bullying prevention programs: A systematic review. *Aggression and Violent Behaviour, 19*, 532–544.

Farrington, D. P. (2003). Methodological quality standards for evaluation research. *The Annals of the American Academy of Political and Social Sciences, 587*, 49–68.

Frey, K. S., Nolen, S. B., Van Schoiack-Edstrom, L., & Hirschstein, M. K. (2005). Effect of a school-based social-emotional competence program: Linking children's goals, attributions, and behavior. *Applied Developmental Psychology, 26*, 171–200.

Frey, K. S., Hirschstein, M. K., Edstrom, L. V., & Snell, J. L. (2009). Observed reductions in school bullying, nonbullying aggression and destructive bystander behavior: A longitudinal evaluation. *Journal of Educational Psychology, 101*, 466–481.

Gall, M. D., Borg, W. R., & Gall, J. P. (1996). *Educational research: An introduction.* White Plains, NY: Longman.

Hess, R. S., & Copeland, E. P. (2001). Students' stress, coping strategies, and school completion: A longitudinal perspective. *School Psychology Quarterly, 16*, 389–405.

Iceland, J. (2006). *Poverty in America: A handbook.* Berkeley, CA: University of California Press.

Ladd, G., & Kochenderfer-Ladd, B. (2002). Identifying victims of peer aggression from early to middle childhood: Analysis of cross-informant data for concordance, estimation of relational adjustment, prevalence of victimization, and characteristics of identified victims. *Psychological Assessment, 14*, 74–96.

Langbeim, L. (2006). *Public program evaluation. A statistical guide.* Armonk, NY: M.E. Sharpe Inc.

Lewis, K. M., DuBois, D. L., Bavarian, N., Acock, A., Silverthorn, N., Day, J., & Flay, B. R. (2013). Effects of positive action on the emotional health of urban youth: A cluster-randomized trial. *Journal of Adolescent Health, 53*(6):706—11. doi: 10.1016/j.jadohealth.2013.06.012.

Li, K.-K., Washburn, I., DuBois, D. L., Vuchinich, S., Ji, P., Brechling, V., & Flay, B. R. (2011). Effects of the Positive Action programme on problem behaviors in elementary school students: A matched-pair, randomized control trial in Chicago. *Psychology & Health, 26*(2), 187–204.

Merton, R. K. (1938). Social structure and anomie. *American Sociological Review, 3*(5), 672–682.

Olweus, D. (1991). Bully/victim problem among school children: Basic facts and effects of a school-based intervention program. In D.J. Pepler & K.H. Rubin (Eds.), *The development and treatment of childhood aggression* (pp. 411–448). Hillsdale, NJ: Erlbaum.

Olweus, D. (1993). *Bullying at school. What we know and we can do.* Oxford, UK: Blackwell.

Olweus, D. (2005). A useful evaluation design, and effects of the Olweus bullying prevention program. *Psychology, Crime & Law, 11*(4), 389–402.

Positive Action Evaluation Report. (2014). Proposed mental health services act—Positive Action evaluation report data from August 2013–June 2014. Retrieved from https://goo.gl/Xvzfsj

Parti K., Schmidt, A., & Néray, B. (2018). Cyberbullying in Hungary. In A. C. Baldry, C. Blaya, D. P. Farrington (Eds.), *International perspectives on cyberbullying*, (pp. 205–229). Cham (Switzerland): Palgrave Macmillan.

Salmivalli, C., Kaukiainen, A., & Voeten, M. (2005). Anti-bullying intervention: Implementation and outcome. *British Journal of Educational Psychology, 75*(2005), 465–487.

Shadish, W., Cook, T., & Campbell, D. (2002). *Experimental and quasi-experimental designs for generalized causal inference.* Boston, MA: Houghton-Mifflin.

Smith P. K., Salmivalli, C., & Cowie, H. (2012). Effectiveness of school-based programs to reduce bullying: A commentary. *Journal of Experimental Criminology, 8*, 433–441.

Smith, J. D., Schneider, B. H., Smith, P. K., & Ananiadou, K. (2004). The effectiveness of whole-school antibullying programs: A synthesis of evaluation research. *School Psychology Review, 33*(4), 547–560.

Smith, P. K., & Shu, S. (2000). What can schools do about bullying: Findings from a survey in English schools after a decade of research and action. *Childhood, 7*, 193–212.

Taub, J. (2001). Evaluation of the Second Step violence prevention program at a rural elementary school. *School Psychology Review, 31*(2), 186–200.

Ttofi, M., & Farrington, D. (2011). Effectiveness of school-based programs to reduce bullying: A systematic and meta-analytic review. *Journal of Experimental Criminology, 7*(2011), 27–56.

Washburn, I. J., Acock, A. C., Vuchinich, S., Snyder, F. J., Li, K. K., Ji, P., & Flay, B. R. (2011). Effects of a social-emotional and character development program on the trajectory of behaviors associated with character development: Findings from three randomized trials. *Prevention Science, 12*, 314–323.

Lightning Source UK Ltd.
Milton Keynes UK
UKHW030635300822
408053UK00007B/802